THE CHRISTIAN IN INDUSTRIAL SOCIETY

D0994758

H. F. R. CATHERWOOD

THE CHRISTIAN IN INDUSTRIAL SOCIETY

LONDON
THE TYNDALE PRESS
39 BEDFORD SQUARE WC1

Printed in Great Britain
by Bookprint Limited
Kingswood and Crawley

CONTENTS

PREFACE

THIS book came into being as a result of a series of discussions between a dozen Christians directly concerned with industry and commerce. From industry and commerce itself we had a company chairman, three managing directors, two directors of research and a banker. All these are senior positions, but our average age was about forty and we had all worked our way up the ladder fairly recently. All of us, including the directors of research, had wide experience in line management. In addition, we had three economists and an official of an Employers' Federation. We had no trade unionist, but we did have the help of Mr George Woodcock, General Secretary of the TUC, in our discussion on the unions, for which we were most grateful. Each discussion was based on a paper by a member and the book is based on the papers, the conclusions of the resultant discussions, and also the further discussion resulting from the publication of some of the findings in *The Christian Graduate*, from June 1962 to June 1963. What is written is not based on the view or experience of one individual. On the other hand, it was felt best that one person should draw the threads together and that it was neither necessary nor desirable to have everyone in the group in agreement with every conclusion in the book.

The main concern of this book is in setting standards for the Christian by applying Christian doctrine to behaviour in society today. But there are also some ways of organizing society itself that are unquestionably helpful to the maintainance of Christian standards and others that are not. We felt that it would be most useful to take two or three chapters to set out the points at issue. In a few key questions we have gone a little further and set out some solutions, not because we felt that they were the only solutions for a Christian, but because we felt the necessity of showing that Christian principles could, in fact, be worked out in a practical way and should not be dismissed as visionary or impractical.

The last chapters of the book deal with our relations with people, those with whom we trade, our employers, our employees and colleagues, and with the particular problems which a Christian faces in working in a society which does not hold strictly to the standards of his own faith.

We have found a remarkable absence of previous study on the subject, and if some conclusions appear to be unsupported or even dogmatic, we can only plead the absence of support, opposition or dogma. To this extent we have had to rely on the experience of the group. We had a fairly wide range of experience and the members of the group held the kind of jobs in which people have to make up their own minds about the problems under discussion.

The regular members of the group were as follows: Mr R. F. Barclay, Dr O. R. Barclay, Mr J. Bunton, the Rt Hon. Viscount Caldecote, Mr H. F. R. Catherwood, Mr J. W. Haig-Ferguson, Mr W. K. Laing, Mr N. de Marchi, Dr M. A. Pickering, Mr P. E. Trier and Dr R. Webb.

Although everyone in the group has taken a great deal of time and trouble in preparing papers, in discussion and in comments on the drafts, especial thanks are due to Dr Oliver Barclay who went through each draft chapter in detail, commenting, amending and, in places, rewriting. Thanks are also due to the Editor of *The Christian Graduate* for permission to reprint chapters 1-4, which originally appeared as articles in that magazine, September 1962 to June 1963; to my wife for her work in making the text lucid, and to Mary Agnew for arranging the meetings and for typing the drafts in addition to a full day in her ordinary job. I must also, on my own behalf, thank my wife for her help and also for her forbearance in looking after three small children alone on the holidays and Saturdays during which this book was written.

INTRODUCTION

THERE would hardly be any argument today against the view that the Christian Church has a diminishing impact on society. The Church itself does not bother to dispute the point. Its time and attention are taken up with the means of re-establishing the contact it appears to have lost. The remedies vary according to the theological position of their exponent. There are those who see their strength in the authority of age-old ritual. Others, in the hope of keeping the Church in fashion, are prepared to make almost every conceivable concession to contemporary philosophy until what is left is unrecognizable as Christianity. Others see the ecumenical movement as the basis of a restored authority. Others continue to preach the 'social gospel', trying to apply the teaching of our Lord to His disciples direct to unregenerate society as if there were no need for personal repentance and forgiveness. The Evangelicals have tended to concentrate almost exclusively on personal evangelism, believing that nothing can be achieved without personal regeneration, and have been prepared to evangelize in complete independence of the Church if they were not free to work within it. As the state of the Church has grown more desperate, Evangelicals have felt increasingly compelled towards this policy. There would seem to be no time for anything but insistence on the key doctrines of personal regeneration and faith.

While there was still a considerable collective impact by Christians in society and while social behaviour was strongly influenced by Christian standards, the evangelical emphasis gave a proper balance. It is now open to question whether the balance is still there and whether Christians should not make more of a collective impact on society than they are doing now. Defensive positions taken up under immediate pressure of events are liable to be unbalanced. Whatever may have been right and necessary at a particular moment, we must ask whether this represents the balance of Christian teaching.

It is true that according to the New Testament accounts personal evangelism was the order of the day in the early Church. But it was done by individual Christians and by a Church whose philosophy and behaviour were both coherent and visibly different from those of the pagan world around.

The Christian testimony to the truth is by both life and word, and in practice the testimony of our lives precedes and provides the occasion for the testimony of our message. The emphasis of the Epistles is overwhelmingly on what we should do rather than on what we should say. People are likely to listen if the sort of life we lead makes them think that there is something worth listening to.

The witness of the individual in word and deed has its place, but it is remarkable how much emphasis there is also on collective witness. That the Corinthian church should condone immoral behaviour is as serious to Paul as the immoral behaviour itself. The witness of the Holy Ghost at Pentecost was through all the church together. Individuals may be written off as cranks. It is not so easy to write off a lively and active church with old and young, men and women, rich and poor, dull and bright, introvert and extrovert, new converts and long-established Christians. It demonstrates that the Christian faith is not just for the individual on his own, but is a way of life affecting men in all their relations with one another. Can we neglect these social implications of Christianity altogether without disobedience to New Testament teaching? If we do so, are we not likely to withdraw into Sunday religion and parlour Christianity, which will not even begin to touch the world around?

This book is written out of the conviction that although the primary responsibility of the Church is to believe and to spread the gospel, it is also essential and not merely optional to try to see how we should obey God in daily life. For all engaged in commerce and industry, particularly in the new and complicated institutions of modern life, this involves special problems. But in solving these problems it also gives the opportunity to set standards for future generations, as past generations of Christians have set standards for us. In this book we shall try to see what obedience to Christian teaching means in some major aspects of industrial society as we know it today.

It is our conviction that the Bible does teach that God cares about the social order. Righteousness, justice, love for the weak and other virtues are not only to be practised in private but, as we are taught in Romans 13, should be a feature of society. But the establishment of codes of social righteousness will not of itself lead anyone into the Christian faith. To concentrate on this to the exclusion of all else is not to preach a balanced gospel either. Men must know what demands God makes on them, but they must realize that these demands are individual before they are collective, they must know the results of disobedience and the way of salvation.

There is, therefore, no 'social *gospel*'. The gospel is addressed to the individual. Society collectively cannot be redeemed. It can, however, be reformed according to the law of God. There is a 'social *law*'. Society in any of its sectors can be made more or less righteous and the Christian must be concerned that, as far as he is able to accomplish it, righteousness shall prevail in those spheres in which he is involved, whether it is a school, a faculty, a local community or a business. To leave them to secularism or humanism would be a complete abdication of our responsibility as Christian citizens.

The preaching and teaching of God's law has two functions. First, it is 'our schoolmaster to bring us to Christ'. It is an essential background to evangelism. Repentance precedes salvation and conviction of sin precedes repentance. The first object of the preacher must be to bring home to men that God's standards are not their standards, and he must do this in terms of the kind of life that they lead, the kind of standards they set and the kind of temptations to which they are prone. Industrial society brings new temptations and requires the setting of new standards. The rural clergyman understood the *mores* of rural society. It is questionable whether the suburban parson has nearly the same close knowledge of what his suburban congregation are up to during the week. Their behaviour on Sunday may be no indication whatever of their relation to their fellow men in the anonymity of the big city or within the closed society of the great corporation. God's law should be made to apply as much in the one place as in the other.

To disagree with the social gospeller's idea that society could be redeemed collectively through good works does not necessarily mean that there is no purpose in applying the moral law to the unbeliever. We may not expect the moral law to produce a society of Christians, but by the preaching of Christian standards and by the work of God's grace we can expect a better society.

The Children of Israel were instructed by both the law and the prophets as to the precise temptations of an agricultural society and their proper behaviour to each other and to strangers. Our Lord does not hesitate to instruct His disciples on their attitude to money, to taxation and to their foreign rulers; and Peter, Paul and James in their Epistles are all concerned with the detailed problems arising from life in a pagan society. Who are we, in our day, to feel that we have no need for such things? And if our Lord was concerned with the earthly needs and sufferings of the society in which He lived, who are we to be indifferent?

The other function of the law is as a means of 'common grace'. This is the grace given by God to the Church and the world alike. God has not given the world over to evil. Even where there is no Christian church and no Christian witness, good is still preserved. The Christian is not yet in heaven, nor is the man of the world in hell. God is still present. His influence is still felt. His Spirit still strives with man. He works through conscience, through the divine institutions of government and family, and perhaps most forcibly of all through the explicit proclamation of God's law by the Church.

Occasionally God has withdrawn this preserving grace. We read of it in the stories of the Flood and of Sodom, and in the first chapter of Paul's Epistle to the Romans. It may be, too, that this is what happened to Jerusalem before it was razed by Titus. God took Noah and Lot away from the society in which each was involved. He warned the Church that the time must come for them to leave Jerusalem to its fate. But while they were there they were to proclaim God's law; and while we are here we too must continue to proclaim God's law and make our contribution to the preservation of the society in which we live.

We are not, as we explain later in the book, expecting to set out a blueprint for a specifically Christian society or company. Indeed it is not at all clear what that would mean. We are concerned to try to explore ways in which explicit biblical teaching and general Christian values work out in these spheres, and how this section of the contemporary world could be made to conform more closely to these Christian ideals.

For society has changed out of all recognition since Christianity attained its last peak of power and influence about a hundred years ago. It has changed radically even since the present pattern of theological positions, parties and movements became established round about the turn of the century. The old social pattern centred round the local community. Half the population a century ago was still agricultural and even the industrial population of a particular town would have been, for the most part, more stable than it is today. More likely than not, people would have lived in the same surroundings and among the same neighbours for most of their lives. Today, the majority of the population of Britain are townsmen, and of these the majority live in huge impersonal conurbations, whose millions scarcely know their neighbours or their workmates. They may change their neighbourhood a number of times in a lifetime and their job a good deal more often. This is the age of a society that is increasingly nomadic and atomized and where even the basic unity of society, the family, is in increasing danger of being split up. There have been many instruments of this change, but the greatest single cause must surely be the power of industrialization which has loosened the narrow confines of traditional society.

Christians cannot disregard these changes. We must set new guide-lines and to do this we must make some judgment on the forces which shape society. This is what Christians have always tried to do in periods of strength and vigour. We cannot limit our views to behaviour on Sunday and in the home. The Reformers took no limited or half-hearted view of society. We cannot imagine an Augustine, a Luther, a Knox, a Hampden, a Wilberforce or Shaftesbury living in our day and declining to express a view on the right and wrong behaviour in the kind of world in which they had to live. To each of these men, there was no problem of morals and behaviour which was beyond the competence of God's Word. They would not have understood the idea that some mysterious and unalterable economic law somehow overrode a Christian's clearly-taught obligations to his neighbour. It is wrong to water down the message of sin, judgment and redemption to a 'do good' social gospel. But it is also wrong to preach as if God's Word is not relevant to men's relations to their fellows, that is to society as we find it.

Those who are always demanding that the Church pronounce on this or that may find this argument somewhat unnecessary, but in this theologically-confused generation there can be no harm in a little definition of one's position.

It should be emphasized that this is not a political pamphlet. This is a book to help Christians to apply the principles of their faith in the society in which they live. It therefore assumes adherence to those principles. It does not presume to tell the humanist or the Jew how to apply his principles. It supposes that those whose faith is different may have different principles and that their conclusions may well be different too. We do believe, however, that Christian principles are the right ones, and that so far as men adhere to them society will be better and so far as they depart from them it will be worse.

It may be that many who read the book may feel that what it says is not specifically Christian, that most of what is advocated could have come just as easily from anyone of high morality, whether Christian or not. Certainly it is no part of our case that there is a different verse from the Bible to solve every different moral problem in a highly complex industrial society. Nor do we claim always to be different from traditional morality. If traditional morality gives the same answers as Christianity, then so much the better for traditional morality. But the Christian must be sure that his behaviour is at least as good as that of traditional morality. Our Lord told His disciples that their righteousness must exceed the righteousness of the scribes and the Pharisees. In fact the morality of a country like Britain owes to Christianity much more than it will now acknowledge, and a good deal of what is best in the moral code of British society has been the working out of Christian morality in practice. In particular, respect for the dignity and responsibility of the individual has been a feature of our society which stems directly from Christian teaching and has been worked out in terms of universal suffrage, universal education and individual liberty. This view of the individual must therefore be part of any Christian view of industrial society. The purpose of this book is to work out the implications in industrial society of the Christian doctrine of the individual, rather than to prove this doctrine all over again to people who substantially accept it.

CHAPTER ONE

THE CHRISTIAN ATTITUDE TO WORK

IN the years following the Reformation it became apparent that there was an essential difference between the developing Protestant ethic and the preceding Catholic ethic in their attitudes to work.[1] This, in turn, seemed to hinge on the difference in their respective attitudes to the natural world around them. The Catholic tended to see the physical world as evil and to him the saint was one who had no part in it. The Catholic saint did not marry or trade. To him, spirituality came by physical withdrawal to holy ground – the monastery and the church – and by external rites. To the Protestant, the evil was within. As our Lord said, 'That which cometh out of the man, that defileth the man.'

The Protestant position was based on the nature of man as unfolded not only by our Lord, but throughout the Bible. The natural resources of the world were created by God and were given to man for his use. 'Let us make man in our image, . . . and let them have dominion over the fish of the sea, and over the fowl of the air, and over the cattle, and over all the earth' (Genesis 1:26). 'And God blessed them, and God said unto them, Be fruitful, and multiply, and replenish the earth, and subdue it: and have dominion . . . over every living thing'(1:28). After the fall of man, the conditions are changed, but the objective is the same. 'In the sweat of thy face shalt thou eat bread' (3:19). The commission which was given to Adam was also given to Noah: 'Be fruitful, and multiply, and replenish the earth. And the fear of you and the dread of you shall be upon every beast of the earth, . . . into your hand are they delivered' (9:1, 2).

We find the same thought in the Psalms of David. 'When I consider thy heavens, the work of thy fingers, the moon and the stars, which thou hast ordained; what is man, that thou art mindful of him?' He then goes on to answer his own question by setting out God's purpose for man on earth. 'Thou madest him to have dominion over the works of thy hands; thou hast put all things under his feet' (Psalm 8:3, 4, 6). Man is a spiritual being, but he has been put on earth to fulfil the purposes of God, and one of these primary and basic purposes is that he should control and

[1] See too Appendix, 'The Weber-Tawney Thesis'.

administer the natural resources of the world. He demonstrates the nature and purpose of God to those who do not believe by obedience to this basic commandment.

If the Christian is to be true to these principles, he does not work simply to make money or to pay the bills. He works because it is part of the divine order that he should work. Even the Christian slave had to remember this: 'Servants, obey in all things your masters according to the flesh; not with eyeservice, as menpleasers; but in singleness of heart, fearing God: and whatsoever ye do, do it heartily, as to the Lord, and not unto men' (Colossians 3:22, 23). Clearly, whatever our work is, we must do it with enthusiasm and not grudgingly or because we are driven to it. It appears to have come more naturally to the early Christians to evangelize than to work, and the exhortation to work is a constant refrain in Paul's Epistles. 'Study to be quiet, and to do your own business, and to work with your own hands, as we commanded you; that ye may walk honestly toward them that are without, and that ye may have lack of nothing' (1 Thessalonians 4:11, 12). Not only must the Christian work, he must work as if for God and he must work whole-heartedly. 'Whatsoever thy hand findeth to do, do it with thy might' (Ecclesiastes 9:10); and our Lord's parable of the talents praises those who made maximum use of their resources and condemns the man who made no use of his because they were small.

It would be fair to deduce from this teaching that it is the duty of the Christian to use his abilities to the limit of his physical and mental capacity. He cannot relax as soon as he has got enough money or as soon as he has mastered his job. He has a duty to train himself and develop his abilities, both academically and experimentally, to the limit that his other responsibilities allow. When he has mastered one job, he should go on to another. He should not be content to administer, but should try to improve and innovate. He should not stop until it is quite clear that he has reached his ceiling.

The Christian who is not called to the ministry should ask, What is God's purpose in life for individual members of the Christian Church? Is it to imitate on a smaller scale and part-time the work of the minister, or is it something separate and different? Too many people today seem to believe that the laity are without functions except those of 'personal evangelist' and part-time preacher. But if we have gifts as evangelists and teachers, why should we not use them full-time? The teaching of the Bible on the function of the laity would appear to be much more positive. The Church is here to glorify God before an unbelieving world by living the kind of life which God intended man to live. It must do what God intended all men to do. It is clear from the passages quoted above that man was intended to control and put to use the untamed resources of the world. To this end he was given powers of intellect and organization. The Christian does not work to earn a living; he works because God intended that he should use the gifts He had given him for the fulfilment of a divine purpose. He goes on working whether or not he needs to earn a living. His work is a divine vocation and not to be treated lightly, whether he is a surgeon or a carpenter. No labour is degrading,

> 'A servant with this clause
> Makes drudgery divine:
> Who sweeps a room, as for Thy laws,
> Makes that and the action fine.'

Ultimately each one of us must decide for himself upon the limits beyond which he cannot stretch his physical and mental powers. He must decide too on the proportion of time and energy he must give to his family and to his spiritual devotions. This is a matter in which extremes are easy and a correct balance difficult. God has laid down that one day in seven should be devoted to Him, and we should go out of our way to see that no secular affairs spill over into that day. The family has a call on our energy and attention as well as our time, and no Christian has a right to allow his work to make his wife a widow or his children orphans.

It is not possible to achieve all these objectives at once without a fair degree of method and self-discipline. These are regarded today as rather old-fashioned virtues, and the modern world seems more concerned with a reduction of stress than with an increase in standards of service. The more complex our work and the less other people can see for themselves what we are doing and why, the more important it is that we should set our own standards. 'The professional must always determine himself what his work should be and what good work is. Neither what he should do, nor what standards should be applied, can be set for him' (Peter Drucker, *The Practice of Management*). The Christian, especially, must organize his life and work, must set his own high standards and must examine the quality of his work continuously and critically against those standards.

It is also important that he should be able to recognize the symptoms of intellectual laziness and lack of self-control so that he can correct them whenever they appear. A man who does his job in a lazy way loses his grip on the situation, and events take charge. Crises begin to arise and he gets into a vicious circle of weariness and worry. In next to no time, he has used up his stock of emotional energy. Had he applied himself to his job in the first place the situation would never have arisen.

Poor personal relationships usually come from lack of self-control and are another great cause of dissipation of emotional energy. There are, of course, people who are particularly difficult, fussy and touchy and we all have to work with them from time to time. But the man who is determined to control his antipathies and who refuses to let people get under his skin, who rides all personal misunderstandings lightly and refuses to take umbrage, will find that he has a good deal more energy left for his job than his more sensitive colleague. But nothing is a greater source of strength than a sense of competence, a feeling that you are on top of the situation and that you have the initiative. It is this which enables men not only to ride out the storm but to have a sense of exhilaration in doing so. This sense of competence is not confined to the Christian, but a Christian who does not feel it, and particularly a Christian who has allowed his job to 'get on top of him', should examine the quality of his work to see whether he has been setting his standards and keeping to them as he ought.

The sloppy thinker will waste hours of his own and other people's time and energy in fruitless fussing. He is full of second-hand ideas and will run everything 'the way we used to run it'. His own ideas are usually half-baked. If he is in charge of others, he will keep them chasing after countless red-herrings and will refuse to see the points he does not want to see.

The man who has trained and disciplined his mind and who is able and willing to use it constructively will think a problem through. He will have the versatility required to examine and assess new evidence. His self-assurance in critical decisions and under pressure of persons and events will be based, not on ignorance or prejudice, but on knowledge. Those who are accustomed to interviewing a great variety of people will know that such men stand out, but they are distinguished not so much by the natural power of their intellect as by its integrity. It is not something with which we are all born but something which most of us can acquire. Many people begin to achieve a tough mental discipline through university or professional examinations in an exact science, but this alone is not enough, and it is necessary to keep the mind at full stretch for several years more before the habit becomes ingrained.

To those who have not faced the problems, stresses and strains of industrial life, these last paragraphs may seem somewhat discursive and academic; but those who have to make critical decisions affecting the material well-being of their fellows will know the misdirections of human effort which can be caused by sloppy thinking. The commonest failing in industrial management today is not that men will not work the hours or the overtime, but that they will not put their minds to work. This is something which a boss may suspect, but which he may find difficult or impossible to bring home. It is something which may take a long time to catch up with us and may indeed never catch up at all – except with our successors!

It is this quality of intellectual integrity which the Christian, above all men, should possess. Our creed is that we are here to serve not ourselves but others; and we should, therefore, be much more conscious than others of our standards of service. The standards we set ourselves should be higher and tougher than others set for us. We should look more closely and critically at our performance than they do. We should put ourselves into the shoes of our boss, our colleagues and our staff and workmen. Seen through their eyes, what do we look like? Industry has its fair share of men who are bogus. What they think when they look at themselves in the mirror is their own business. But there is a large grey area in which men are capable of deceiving themselves as to their true worth and performance, and at the very least the Christian should examine himself to see that he is setting himself high standards and keeping to them. Too often the Christian is no better than the next man.

While high standards and an honest mind are essential, we should not belittle the value of sheer hard work. Long hours alone are not enough, but the Christian is called to use his talents to the full, to work with all his might, to run the race of life as if there were only one prize and he must obtain it. A race is not run, it is true, in a flat-out spurt, but it does require determination and endurance, the ability to keep going when others have stopped and the reserves for the spurt when occasion demands it. All this sounds melodramatic, of course, to the man of the world, a little unnecessary and liable to spoil a man's health and his enjoyment of the natural pleasures of life. But those whose lives and happiness are dependent on the results of our work do not see it in that way. The men in the works and their families depend on us to find the markets to keep them in employment, and to maintain the level of technical expertise and efficiency which will keep their firm competitive. They do not grudge the manager his necessary relaxation, but they know the difference between a management which is working and one which is cruising. The Christian should be the man who is known in the jargon as 'the self-starter'. He does not require pushing, he hardly needs supervision. He goes straight for the tough problem and breaks it. When a critical decision has to be made, he is the man who will have done his homework. He may not, of course, be an attractive character in society. We can exaggerate the antipathy of the educated Englishman to the ideal of hard work, but dedicated as many of them may have been to duty and public service, the image of the gentleman as a man of leisure has gained sufficient respectability to be an ideal to many people who ought to know better.

Today there seems to be a feeling that we are reaching saturation point in personal wealth and that soon we ought to invest not in goods, but in leisure. Whatever others may decide for themselves, this attitude would seem to be wrong for a Christian. The excessively long hours of the past were onerous and made it difficult for a man to carry out his responsibilities to his family and his church. But working hours now are not normally unreasonable and there can be no case for sitting back when there is so much want in the world. Even in this country, the care of the aged, medicine and education are almost bottomless pits, and it will be a long time before their needs are satisfied. Abroad, hundreds of millions are living at no more than subsistence level, and many of these primary-producing countries are dependent on a high and rising level of activity in the industrial nations for any increase in their own low standard of living. 'Trade, not aid' is their slogan. In fact they need both aid and trade. In a country like Northern Rhodesia a slight drop in the price of copper due to falling demand can wipe out a whole year's revenue in aid funds. However, our duty to work arises from clear and explicit instructions in the Bible and not indirectly through our duty to our neighbour. Many of those who first followed the Protestant ethic had long since satisfied their own small personal needs. In an age when poverty was regarded as an ineradicable evil, they went on working regardless, because the Bible told them that this was right. It is just as well for us that they did.

It is worth pausing for a moment to look at the various traditional attitudes towards work and business which have become woven into our society, because we are influenced by them in more ways than we might suspect, so that Christians coming from different backgrounds are too often more influenced by those backgrounds than by their common faith. The original 'Protestant ethic' is perhaps seen in its purest form in the Scottish attitude to work and education. The Scots seem to apply themselves to work and self-development with more whole-hearted zeal than the Englishman and, though it might be difficult to prove, they seem to be more successful in business and the professions, for their numbers, than the English. Until recently a much higher proportion of Scots went to university. The Scottish educational system can be traced to the Reformation and to John Knox in particular.

In England, the Reformation was less thorough and the tradition of the country was not broken as cleanly as in Scotland. South of the border there remained, side by side with the attitudes which arose from the Reformation, attitudes which remained medieval and aristocratic in their lineage. It would clearly be foolish to try to fit all the pattern of English life into two tight straitjackets or to father every attitude today on one of these two traditions. Both had much that was good and much that was bad. But although the older line of thought contained a high sense of personal duty and much else that was good, it contained little or nothing of the duty to work. A gentleman might be called upon to lead, but he was not called upon to work. It was not the aristocracy of England which was responsible for the Scientific and Industrial Revolutions.

This attitude has been modified outwardly under pressure of public opinion, backed by political power which was previously lacking. But it is still apparent in many unexpected places. A country which sends so few of its best-educated young men into industry and trade, when it depends on these for its very existence, must have compelling reasons. The country whose social leaders invented the Long Weekend may be thought to be less than whole-hearted in its attitude to work. These things should put us on our guard and should perhaps cause some of us to examine, critically and from first principles, the traditions in which we have been educated and the influences which have affected those traditions.

Hard work and education were as much part of the tradition of Methodism as they were of the Scots Presbyterians, and Methodism had a great influence on working-class men. Professor Postan thought that their application to their work was one of the main forces of the Industrial Revolution and one of the factors, therefore, which enabled this country to pull itself up by its bootstraps. However, the force of Methodism has waned and has been replaced by the traditions of organized labour. Not all of these can be traced to Christian sources. Many of them stem from a feeling of genuine grievance at the sufferings of the working class. They saw these as arising from a system which appeared to regard labour as a commodity rather than a calling. Indeed the Church's apparent connivance in this system of society, which seemed detrimental to the interests of the individual, may be one of the reasons why the masses are outside the Church today.

The British tradition which appears to reflect the Protestant ethic most strongly is the code of the professional man. In our law, our medicine, our civil service, our armed forces, we have a tradition of professional competence, public duty, disinterested service and financial integrity which it is difficult to better anywhere else in the world. Sometimes this professional code is incorporated in the rules of the professional institutions, but more often it is a tradition which is handed down from generation to generation. This tradition engenders the mutual confidence which is necessary to enable men to trust others with their interests. It is a cement which binds society together, but because it works so well we hardly notice it. It is only when we go to countries which have no such traditions – and unfortunately there are only too many of them – that we realize the damage to the fabric of society which results from the lack of such standards. It may seem too much to claim such a close correlation between the Christian faith and standards of professional conduct, but it is in the Christian and Protestant countries that these standards are most commonly found, and every Christian who is a professional man will agree that his faith and his professional standards go hand in hand.

It is the duty of each generation to re-examine its attitudes by Christian standards, and it is to be hoped that we, in our generation, may rediscover the sense of purpose which a Christian should have in his earthly vocation and the sense of harmony which we should have with the world which God created for our use.

CHAPTER TWO

THE CHRISTIAN ATTITUDE TO WEALTH

THIS attitude to work on the part of the Christian results very often in a substantial increase in wealth. It is noteworthy that the Bible does not condemn wealth in itself. It is not money, but 'the love of money', which is the root of all evil. The fruits of the earth are the gift of God and not to be despised. The bounty of nature is there to be used and there is enough for all if only we have energy enough to lay claim to it. It may be that God uses poverty to bring men to a sense of spiritual reality and it may be that some men, like the apostles, are called to a life of poverty; but poverty brings suffering and great distress and this cannot be an end in itself. The posters of Oxfam have lately brought this home to us in a most direct and compelling way.

The teaching of the Bible would appear to be that it is not the amount of a man's wealth which matters; what matters is the method by which he acquires it, how he uses it and his attitude of mind towards it. Paul tells Timothy, 'Charge them that are rich in this world, that they be not high-minded, nor trust in uncertain riches, but in the living God, who giveth us richly all things to enjoy; that they do good, that they be rich in good works, ready to distribute, willing to communicate' (1 Timothy 6:17, 18). Paul has a positive attitude to the good things which God has given us, because they are from God. He does not try to curb our worldliness by belittling God's provision for us. Instead he teaches that we must share our possessions and here, as elsewhere in both Old and New Testaments, we are taught to rely not on material possessions, but upon God. Nor are we to set our mind on riches. As Paul tells Timothy earlier in the same Epistle, 'Godliness with contentment is great gain. For we brought nothing into this world, and it is certain we can carry nothing out. And having food and raiment let us be therewith content. But they that will be rich fall into temptation and a snare, and into many foolish and hurtful lusts, which drown men in destruction and perdition. For the love of money is the root of all evil.'

These temptations are common to rich and poor alike. If we are poor we must not become obsessed by the desire to become rich. If we are rich, we must sit lightly to our riches. James tells us that the rich man must 'rejoice . . . in that he is made low: because as the flower of the grass he shall pass away' (1:10). He must take care that his temporary riches do not make him arrogant because he and his riches will both shortly perish.

Throughout the Bible there are passages dealing with the wrongful acquisition of wealth. We have, of course, the specific and overriding commandment, 'Thou shalt not steal.' Jeremiah pronounces 'Woe unto him that buildeth his house by unrighteousness, and his chambers by wrong; that useth his neighbour's service without wages, and giveth him not for his work' (22:13). James condemns those who use their riches to oppress the poor (2:6) and those who keep back the wages of their labourers (5:4).

We are forbidden to increase our wealth by the oppression of those whose poverty makes them defenceless. The possession of wealth has traditionally given power to its possessors. In agricultural countries, this power is exercised by the concentration of the great estates in the hands of the wealthy families. Where there is no alternative employment, those who are without means have to work on the terms offered by the wealthy. In these conditions, it is clearly wrong to use this power to exact terms which do not give the employee the wages which are available as a result of his labour. I should have thought it equally wrong to aggregate wealth with the purpose of improving one's economic bargaining position as an employer, or to take steps which would weaken the independence of one's labour force. There is usually sufficient alternative employment in industrial countries to strengthen the power of the poor to resist oppression by the rich. But in an industrial as opposed to an agricultural community, the alternative of self-employment as a craftsman or a small-holding peasant is not normally available, and where there is oppression it is liable to be much more severe. Any government purporting to act on Christian principles should, therefore, aim to protect the citizen against concentration of economic power and should take positive steps to ensure that the citizen has plenty of alternative sources of employment. Any employer acting on Christian principles should co-operate with such a policy. We might note in passing that a concentration of industrial power in the hands of the state does not, of itself, guarantee that the state will not use its monopoly position wrongfully.

The object of the Bible's prohibition of usury seems to be similar. In a country of small-holdings a crop failure could be disastrous for the farmer who did not have some ready resources to tide him over. In these circumstances, those who held the resources could hold to ransom those who did not, and force them, by rates of interest in excess of the earning power of the property, either to mortgage their property or to sell it. The right thing to do in the circumstances was to help your neighbour over a bad patch and not to take advantage of him. This abuse is quite different from the present practice of charging interest at a rate which can be covered adequately by earnings. But the principle can still be applied today. No-one should exploit his neighbour's misfortune. The use of one's capital to do this is still wrong. Wealth is a trust to be used for our neighbour's good and not to his harm.

Perhaps the most odious method of making money is to trade on men's spiritual fears and desires. Money made in this way is denounced as 'filthy lucre' by both Paul (1 Timothy 3:3; Titus 1:7) and Peter (1 Peter 5:2). The elder who rules well and the teaching elder must not only be paid but are worthy of 'double honour' (1 Timothy 5:17). Nevertheless, church leaders must serve without thought of financial gain. In the present penurious conditions of the Christian churches in this country this is perhaps not a very pressing temptation, but in other days and in other lands preachers have been known to pitch their message to suit the frame of mind of their wealthier supporters. From this to the selling of indulgences is only a matter of degree.

Most men in business are interested in their personal power in their own company. They want security, freedom of action and the least number of awkward questions. In the great public companies, with net assets worth tens and hundreds of millions of pounds, personal wealth is normally too small to be a factor in the balance of power within the company. At the other extreme, the private company is directly controlled by its owners. In between is a growing area where directors hold a minority interest and, by means of these personal holdings, control the company. In the case of a company with many small individual holdings outside the board, it is rare for more than 15 per cent of the shareholders to reply to a proxy vote, so that unless something appears to be obviously wrong, a board holding of 20 per cent is adequate for control. Even in a critical situation, a board holding of 35 per cent is normally considered unassailable.

There is obviously something to be said for a director having a stake in the business which he is directing, and much good has come from the sense of trust which generations of the same family have had towards the business they have built up. There is little doubt that the worst abuses of capitalist theory have been avoided because the owner of a business could decide that, for the sake of his workforce, he would not exact the maximum profit from his business. Businesses which are family-controlled are not in danger of involuntary take-over by those who want the maximum return. While the threat of take-over remains and while companies are socially accountable only to a limited extent, the conscientious owner will feel obliged to hold on to his shares for the sake of his employees, and the less conscientious owner will hold on for his own sake. But if there were some social and political accountability, if the owner could be assured that, when he gave up his guardianship, other competent hands would take it up, there is much to be said for the diminishing of unfettered personal control. Complete personal power over a small business of 100 people is unlikely to go to anyone's head, but personal power over an empire of 5,000 people is another matter. Recently the 88-year-old Chairman of a £100m. company with thousands of employees was succeeded as Chairman by another member of the family aged 24. It may be that both were the best possible members of the whole enterprise to be Chairman, but one is entitled to doubt it. Directors are in charge of the country's means of production. In so far as they understand the expensive and complex instruments under their control and use their full potential, the country will prosper and will be able to help and defend less fortunate countries. In so far as they use their power to neglect the dull or difficult, but important, jobs in favour of jobs which may be fascinating, but are relatively unimportant, or have around them people who are congenial instead of people who are competent, they diminish the wealth otherwise available to the whole community.

Wealth is not always used to buy power. It can also be used for self-indulgence and ostentatious display. It is clearly wrong for the Christian to use it in this way. What is not always so clear is where the line is to be drawn. Increasing wealth brings increasing obligations, and it is only too easy for those who do not have the obligations to criticize the establishment and expenditure of those who do. A recurring theme of the New Testament is that Christians, especially Christian leaders, should be 'given to hospitality'. This is a quite specific obligation to those Christians who have more than the average share of worldly goods, and life would be the poorer if every Christian limited his establishment and table to cater for himself and his immediate family. Most Christians who have been students or strangers remember with gratitude some Christian household where they were made to feel at home, where they made friends with other Christians or even made their first encounter with Christianity. The Christian is not told to be without worldly goods, but he is told to share with those who are less fortunate such worldly goods as he has.

The Christian, however, ought to be different in the way he spends his money. Certainly there seems to be no case for Christian expenditure on extravagances which vary from generation to generation, but now go under the title of 'status symbol'. The essence of this type of expenditure seems to be that its price exceeds its intrinsic worth on account of utility or beauty because it confers prestige on its owner. The Christian need not live between the gasworks and the linoleum factory if he can afford to live somewhere more salubrious, but he almost certainly should not spend three times as much as he need on a house just because a temporary fashion has created an insatiable demand for mews and workmen's cottages in SW3. It is not necessary for the Christian woman to be dowdy, but neither is it necessary for her to order all her dresses from Paris. It is right that a Christian should want a good education for his children, but it is almost certainly wrong for him to spend money in having his children educated in purely snobbish values. While some Christian values remain in society, the Christian will not appear other than abstemious and unextravagant. It is only when society or some classes in society have thrown over Christian values that the Christian who has to live among them may be thought cranky. But it is worth bearing in mind that although Wilberforce and the Clapham Sect may have been thought odd by Regency society, it was the Evangelicals and not Beau Brummell who had the most lasting influence on English social standards for the next half-century.

There is no logical reason why the Christian should not have a perfectly sober and sensible attitude to money, but the warnings in the Bible indicate that this is not as easy as it appears. Only one of the succeeding nine commandments is said to be a breach of the first and greatest commandment. In both Ephesians 5 and Colossians 3 we are told that covetousness is idolatry.

Our Lord has told us that the first and greatest commandment is to love the Lord our God with all our heart and mind and soul and strength. If we make an idol of wealth, we put it in God's place and this is a breach of the first commandment. It is, therefore, a sin we should take particular precautions to avoid. There are two dangerous features to this sin; one is that it is respectable, the other that hardly anyone is ever aware of committing it. A Roman Catholic priest once said that he had heard confessions to every known sin except the sin of covetousness.

In view of its seriousness and subtlety it might seem that the wealthy Christian was justified in taking quite specific measures to avoid temptation, by putting beyond the reach of his personal enjoyment such capital and income as was not required to provide an income for himself and his family should he become incapacitated. Some Christians have, in fact, done this. In one case it was done by outright gifts of part of the capital to various causes and the transfer of another part to a charitable trust set up for the purpose by the donor. In cases where the whole capital has been given away without any provision for the family, relatives who were often not Christians have been left to pay the bills for family disasters and even for education of children. This is not a case for going to dramatic extremes, but for quietly drawing a line at a certain point, for putting the temptations of wealth firmly and irrevocably aside.

Most of us, however, are not wealthy or ever likely to be, and our temptations may not be so easily overcome. Poverty does not exempt a man from the sin of covetousness. It was not to the rich that Paul wrote, 'Be content with such things as ye have'. The problems of covetousness exist for every Christian. We must agree that there is nothing wrong in material possessions. A comfortable home, a garden, holidays, machines which take the drudgery out of housework, enjoyment of music – all these are good in themselves and are not to be despised. The man who works to give his family these material benefits and to provide for the future does nothing wrong. A man must provide for those of his own household (1 Timothy 5:8) and the parents lay up for the children (2 Corinthians 12:14). But we must do so by honest work and not by preferring our claims over those of others, or by exploiting a shortage of our particular skill. The Christian businessman should try to make the maximum profits only where profits are a true economic regulator and he should not maximize profits where to do so would be to exploit his special power over the worker or the customer. A better objective would be the maximization of economic performance to give the best value to the customer, the shareholder and the worker. Only if the customer and worker have the sanction required to support their own interests will maximization of profits and maximization of economic performance amount to the same thing.

Where a Christian is considering alternative jobs, he clearly should not allow the material reward to be the primary consideration. In some cases he will find that a higher salary is offered to offset the lower standing of the firm making the offer or the uninteresting or insecure nature of the job. On the other hand, between firms of equal standing, salary is a measure of the worth of the job and a Christian who sees a higher salary being offered for a job for which he is qualified is not being covetous if he puts in for it. He is right, all else being equal, to go where his services are of most value.

The Christian's overriding rule is that he should sit lightly to worldly wealth. If he disciplines himself to do this, if he avoids setting his heart on any material possession, if he can contemplate the loss of possessions with equanimity and regard their possession as a matter of indifference, then he will be less likely to fall prey to the sin of covetousness. He should increasingly realize the truths that 'moth and rust . . . corrupt, and . . . thieves break through and steal', that he came naked into the world and must depart naked out of it. Above all he should grasp the contrast between this world and the world to come. The saints, who in this world were 'tortured . . . stoned . . . sawn asunder . . . slain with the sword . . . destitute, afflicted, tormented; (of whom the world was not worthy)' and who 'wandered in deserts, and in mountains, and in dens and caves of the earth', will in the world to come receive their final reward. The man of the world does not believe in this 'pie in the sky', and no more does the humanist. The Christian should be no less anxious than the humanist to relieve poverty and misery in this world and in doing so he will follow his Master's example. But if a man professes to be a Christian and does not believe that God will finally perfect His creation, and if he believes that 'the dead rise not', then, Paul tells him, Christ is not raised; 'and if Christ be not raised, your faith is vain'. If he believes these truths, the Christian will sit lightly to this world and its passing benefits. His possessions here will be incidental and he will be more open-handed with them. He will find no insuperable obstacle to giving the Church its tithe or more than its tithe. He will not press his claims on scarce resources to the damage of his neighbour, and he will not be guilty of the sin of covetousness, which is idolatry.

CHAPTER THREE

ECONOMICS, POLITICS AND THE CHRISTIAN

THIS is the age of the economist. It is the age in which all our debate is centred on the relative merits of different economic systems. Are we for communism or capitalism? Are we for or against planning? Is sterling over- or undervalued? Will socialism give a faster rate of economic growth? Should we go into the Common Market? These are the broad points of public discussion and provoke much impassioned argument on all issues, major and minor. Indeed, the medieval disputations on the number of angels which could stand on the point of a needle are nothing to the more esoteric arguments of modern economists. Both disputations have in common that certain fundamental information is always missing, and as a result no-one can ever prove his point.

Economics is about means and not about ends. It is concerned with the relation between resources and wants. It is not concerned with the technology by which the resources are developed, nor is it concerned with the ethical standards used in deciding priorities for the satisfaction of wants. It aims simply to match given resources to given demands in the most economic manner. Of course some economists, like some scientists, are given to pronouncing on moral and ethical matters outside their own particular expertise and are not immune from allowing their political prejudices to colour their economic judgments. But economics, as economics, is a science not concerned directly with morals or politics. In deciding on its impact on Christian values – and it does have an impact – we need to distinguish between the economic system as such and the political system which sanctions or enforces it. The tendency today is to give blanket denunciation or support to the combined political and economic system of a country. It is true that a particular economic system and a particular political system may seem to be interdependent and sometimes it may be difficult to distinguish them, but if we are to pass moral judgments, we must make this effort.

The different forms of economic organization can be broadly distinguished from each other in the way in which they own their means of production and the way in which they co-ordinate them. Under pure communist economics, resources are centrally owned and centrally co-ordinated. Under pure capitalist economics, ownership and co-ordination are decentralized. In war-time economy or emergency conditions resources may be centrally controlled while ownership remains decentralized. Under traditional socialist economics, ownership is centralized, but large areas of co-ordination remain decentralized. Of course this is an over-simplified picture. All kinds of practical pressures have modified the purity of these economic doctrines. Most socialists do not now believe in the central ownership of all 'the means of production, distribution and exchange'. Nor can most communists believe that every single com-modity can be centrally planned and distributed without the use of the price mechanism. Capitalists are now moving towards the idea that central planning has its place in the system. Consequently most economies are a mixture of the four basic patterns.

This broad classification does not exhaust the possibilities. Even where there is no centralized public ownership of resources, it is still possible to have centralized private ownership if one company obtains a mono-poly; and even where there is no centralized public direction, it is still possible to have centralized private direction by agreement between the companies in the industry. It is also increasingly common to have central-ized ownership with a large degree of decentralized direction. Group-holding companies operate in this way, as do some co-operatives. There is, therefore, a very large variety of methods of economic organization which can be put together in a considerable number of different com-binations; and they are not necessarily put in the same combinations by supposedly similar political systems. It may well be that a particular combination under a dictatorial political system would be harmful to Christian values, while the same combination under a democracy would be beneficial. A democracy can agree to put the economy under central direction in war-time, and much good may come from the realization of common purposes and interests. But a dictator can use central direction to maintain himself in power and to suppress individual liberties.

What are these values which the Christian should wish to promote and preserve in economic and political life? What are the harmful tendencies against which the Christian should be particularly on his guard? Two doctrines guide him. One, that man was made in the image of God and is individually accountable to God for all his acts. The other, that he is responsible for his fellows. He is to love both God and his neighbour.

The Christian, above all men, respects the dignity of the individual. He may be even more conscious than others of the baser sides of human nature. But this brings him to have compassion on his fellows, and not to despise them. 'There, but for the grace of God, go I.' He can still see, through all the degradation, something of the original image of the Creator. He can see the possibilities of transformation, even in this life, to something better and more worthy. He knows the power of God to change the most debased man or woman into a saint. He knows that contempt of his fellows is a sin. He believes that the Son of God was 'despised and rejected of men'. He understands that he must love even his enemies. To the Christian, no-one is outside the pale. No man, however degraded and however hostile, can be dismissed as of no account. Onesimus the slave had as much standing before God as Philemon the master. Although the apostles did not directly challenge the existing structure of society, their teaching made it impossible for slavery to continue side by side with a devoted and effective Christian Church. This teaching of the dignity and responsibility of the individual cannot be safely divorced from specifically Christian doctrine. When it is so divorced, the 'rights of man' tend to become the rights of society, society becomes an end in itself and the individual has been sacrificed to the will of the state. The Christian, like the humanist, may believe that a man is wrong-headed and anti-social; but, unlike some humanists, he should not endeavour to coerce him. If he has broken the law, the Christian believes that he should be given the punishment which justice demands of a responsible individual, because 'the powers that be are ordained of God', but would be chary of attempts to treat him as an irresponsible member of society who must be conditioned to the view of the majority. Although the Christian believes his views to be right and believes in his right to put these views, his respect for the individual must extend to those who disagree with him.

The duty of compassion and care for our brother and our neighbour is taught from beginning to end of the Bible. The second commandment is that we should love our neighbour as ourself. This is second only to our duty to love God. In the story of the good Samaritan, our Lord makes it clear that anyone who crosses our path can be considered to be our neighbour. Our Lord, when commissioning the disciples, gave them the whole world as their charge. Paul tells the Galatians, 'As we have therefore opportunity, let us do good unto all men, especially unto them who are of the household of faith.'

While the Christian is concerned for the freedom and the good of others, he is also very concerned that society should be so organized that men can practise and preach their faith without persecution or coercion. He is much more sensitive than the man of the world to the possibilities of coercion, and he is more aware of the force of intolerance beneath the thin veneer of official tolerance. He is normally better informed on the broad areas in the world today where men are still imprisoned and out-lawed for their faith and where the preaching of the Christian gospel is an offence. For all these reasons, the Christian will be reluctant to see too much concentration of power, including economic power. Christians have known the reality of the vision of the apostle John, 'no man might buy or sell, save that he had the mark, or the name of the beast'. The price of liberty is eternal vigilance, and in an age when the loss of a union card may spell disaster for a man in one of the most tolerant countries in the world, this vigilance is more than ever necessary.

Before we look at the various broad systems of economic organization past and present, we ought to put down some general standards arising out of Christian doctrine against which they may be judged.

The essential economic freedom is the right of a man to change his job. So long as he can both leave his job and also find another without hard-ship, he retains a high degree of personal freedom. If his employer wishes to keep him, he is bound to treat him with respect. But as soon as the situation arises in which a man cannot leave without severe penalties, his liberty disappears and he becomes subservient in greater or lesser degree. In countries where the worker is free to form unions and is entitled to the sanction of withdrawing his labour without fear of reprisal, he is, to a large extent, protected against the whims of the employer (though not always against the whims of the union). For this reason the unions are a very real form of protection, and it is interesting to compare the kind of country where unions have a privileged position with those where they do not.

The person most seriously affected today by the power of the employer is the non-unionized worker, particularly the unqualified and older manager. The qualified manager has a universally-accepted credential which enables him to transfer easily to another post. The younger manager, though unqualified, does not find it too difficult in times of full employment to obtain another job. But the manager over forty-five without any qualification except his experience may not be in a position to argue too much with his boss. Even if he finds someone else who wants him, he cannot normally leave without sacrificing a substantial part of his pension and, because of high taxation, he is not normally in a position where he is independent of his pension. It is surprising how few people in a large corporation are really independent. Even the executive director will think twice before he falls out with the managing director or the

C·

chairman. The reason for this is that in the case of most large companies the shareholders do not exercise any effective control over the board, and there is no countervailing check on the power of the two or three men in control.

It would seem that Christian principles of economic freedom for the employee are best met by a diffusion of economic power. Unless there are very special reasons for it, the Christian would prefer, from this point of view, not to see either private or state monopoly. In both cases the individual may well find himself in a position where disagreement with authority prevents him from exercising the skills in which he has been trained, because there is only one employer who can use his skill. It is most unlikely that one body of men is possessed with all the wisdom; and it is desirable that other bodies, possessed of the same intimate knowledge of a complex industry, should be following alternative methods and ideas. It is likely that if an industry is confined to one point of view there will be a large number of people who are in conflict with authority. The Christian may well be among their number, because he is unlikely to take the cynical view, 'if that's what they want, that's what they will get'. His sense of vocation will give him separate standards, which may make him less complaisant than the average employee. He is, therefore, more concerned than many men with the right to resign if the requirements of his job and his own standards of work are incompatible.

This difficulty is not, of course, confined to Christians, but is encountered by anyone with professional standards of work. It would be satisfactory to be able to say that such conflicts could never arise in a state-owned monopoly, but this would not be true. Certainly the difficulties inherent in a capitalist monopoly do not arise, but the state monopoly has its own particular difficulties in addition to those which arise throughout industry. These difficulties are far from being imaginary, and unfortunately the trend in industry is bringing them into even sharper relief. The big organization is making demands on men's loyalty which it has no right to make. This is very well summarized in a letter to *The Times* at the time of the ICI bid for Courtaulds: 'Under the debilitating surveillance of paternalistic personnel departments and with no effective court of appeal, few junior members of large industrial staffs have the private resources to back their judgment in any dispute, and anxieties over fixed outgoings on homes and families coupled with the difficulty of transferring at all rapidly to another equally paying job, reinforce company discipline to a most unhealthy degree.' Unfortunately this does not stop at junior members of staff. The higher up the scale you go, the more difficult it is to find another comparable job. One of the junior directors of Courtaulds made it clear that the junior directors had no effective say in the lowering of the Courtaulds' dividend immediately preceding the ICI bid. Had they resigned, they would have lost their livelihood and might well have been labelled as 'controversial' and found it exceedingly hard to find another post. But if capitalism is far from perfect, it does give at least the freedom to change, whereas where the state is the sole employer the individual loses a very real freedom.

The Christian might well consider that it was essential to economic freedom that everyone should be left with some money which he could spend as he liked, so that he could have some say in the way he lived and, as a Christian, provide an income for the Church. It is undesirable that the Church should depend on the state for its income. There are one or two countries where it has done so with no apparent ill effect, but as a matter of principle it would seem wrong for the state to be the paymaster of the Church and much more in accord with biblical principles that Christians should support it directly. This means that, other things being equal, the Christian would not advocate an economic system where the worker was paid in kind, and had no funds left, over which he had personal discretion. It does not mean that we should insist on diverting to private charity substantial funds which otherwise would go to tax revenue. In the UK, at present, there is rather a nice balance. A taxpayer can divert funds to private charity if he is prepared to do so for a period which may exceed six years (the seven-year covenant) and provided he is prepared to pay surtax on the whole of his income. Only at standard rate is the whole of his income diverted. This last provision provides an effective ceiling to the proportion of his income he can divert and is necessary to prevent large portions of the country's surtax ending up in homes for stray cats and like beneficiaries of private enthusiasms. Although the Christian might like the arrangements to be more generous, it is hard to see how this could be done without opening the way to abuse.

In many parts of the world society, even today, is so organized that the surplus left to the individual in freely negotiable form is tiny, and he has scarcely any opportunity to establish a pattern of life independently of his employer. There must be a balance between individualism and discipline, and individualism can run riot; but man was created in the image of God and not in the image of the beasts. If some men have lost their dignity and individuality and seem to have lost their creative powers, if they run in a herd like animals, that is because they have fallen from their original estate. We must try to organize society so that they can be lifted up again. Uniforms and barracks may be necessary in a fallen society, but they are not part of the Christian's ideal for mankind.

If we are to preserve the individual's economic freedom in this day and age, he must not only have an income in cash rather than in kind, he must also have free access to essential goods and services. It should be impossible for any sanction to be imposed against him by the cutting off of essential supplies. In many places, for instance, the only housing available to the working man may be in the gift of the local council. Cases have been known where candidates for trade union or municipal office who also hold appointments on local councils have had it made clear to their rivals that, if they do not withdraw, their chances of obtaining a council house are remote. Fortunately this sort of thing is rare, but although local government housing does give good housing at low rents, it is not desirable that all housing should be in the gift of the government.

For this reason we should insist that the supply of essential goods be carried on through a number of different channels so that there is no possibility of discrimination by the state, by powerful interests or even by petty officialdom. Because discrimination has not happened in this country in living memory, it may be thought that it is of minor importance here. Most of us are capable of standing up for ourselves, and there is a strong British habit of protest if petty officialdom appears to overreach itself. The best forms of protection are, of course, our democratic system of government and the rule of law. The former makes our rulers answerable for their conduct and the latter guards against discrimination; but in these days of specialization, when we are so dependent on our fellow men in all we do, the possibilities of discrimination are all too many.

One has a feeling in reading about past persecutions that they faded out largely through inefficiency and administrative difficulties. In our tightly knit and closely organized society, there would be small hope of this. Were there to be some falling off in the standards of official impartiality, a weakening in political standards or a strong popular feeling against minorities, the latter could very quickly find themselves in a corner. This deterioration is not at all impossible. We owe more than most people will admit to the moral standards of previous generations, largely inspired by Christian teaching. The teaching has been thrown over and standards of morals and tolerance are visibly deteriorating. We hope that it will go no further, but concentrations of economic power are difficult to pull apart and it seems just as well that they should not be built.

Most governments today have as their avowed objective the highest possible standard of living for all their people. This would seem a proper objective for the Christian. If we believe that the world was given us by God for our use, and that we were given the intellect to use its resources and the command to work, then poverty would seem to be a curse which it should be our aim to eradicate. Whatever their demerits in other directions, this is the avowed objective of both communism and socialism, and it is to this that they owe their popularity, particularly in the under-developed parts of the world. This is not and never has been an objective of feudalism, and in so far as 'pure' and 'unrestrained' capitalism is a mechanical system without political objectives, the relief of poverty would be an incidental rather than a declared objective.

Since the publication of Professor Galbraith's book *The Affluent Society* in 1958, there has been much misinformed talk about the subject. It seems to be accepted that Galbraith has proved that all Western society has now reached a dangerous degree of affluence and that it should cease to aim at higher prosperity. Those who have taken the trouble to read Galbraith's book will realize, however, that his argument is more local and specialized. He deals almost exclusively with the USA. The over-all American standard of living is away beyond any other standard of living in the world. Galbraith argues that at this point – a point which no-one else has reached – the Americans might recognize that the manufacture and promotion of consumer goods had been overdone and that they might have taxes on the sale of non-essential goods, like the British purchase tax, to finance better public services, such as a public health service and local authority housing (neither of which they have).

Of course, living standards in Britain have risen markedly in the last twenty or thirty years, but the high wages now paid to teenagers and the good housing available to those who have had their name down for long enough on the council list mask the poor conditions in which millions in Britain still live. It ill becomes those who feel that their middle-class comforts are a minimum necessity to declare that the working classes now have enough. It is also unreasonable for those whose fathers paid for an expensive education to deride the tastes and mental ability of those who were educated in classes of forty and who had to leave school at fifteen. The economic advance of all classes is relatively recent and, in a competitive world, relatively precarious. It is difficult to feel that we have yet reached the age when an increased national standard of living ceases to be a proper Christian objective.

Believing as he does in the dignity of the individual, the Christian must qualify the objective of economic growth by saying that this should be pursued by persuasion and not by force. This qualification is important because inertia and encrusted habit are the largest single obstacles to economic growth and it is tempting, particularly in under-developed countries, to try to sweep them out of the way. In an agricultural country, it may be obvious to the rulers that farming with small-holdings is inefficient and uneconomic and will never bring the country's production of food up to the level required to give reasonable standards for the industrial worker. At this point it is tempting to put through a forced collectivization to ensure that farms are mechanized and run as economic units. A government which does not respect the dignity of the individual will take this short cut, justifying the means by the greater good of the majority which will shortly result. This kind of action may well be ineffective and self-defeating, but even if it were effective, it would seem wrong arbitrarily to uproot an individual from a settled way of life. The majority has no right to demand this of the minority.

Over the years, ways have been worked out of overcoming the obstruction of the minority in ways which respect their existing position, but remove it as an obstacle to progress. The first principle is that if they cannot be persuaded to change their habits to help the majority, they should be given some financial inducement to change. Customers may not like the idea of a self-service store, and the idea of saving scarce national manpower may mean nothing to old Mrs Oakley of Victoria Terrace, Gateshead; but when Mrs Oakley finds that she can get more for her money at the self-service, she is made to place a value on her gossip with the shop assistants, and eventually she will decide that it is not worth it. The men in No. 2 Bay may not see why they should change their working habits because the young work study engineer has come up with some bright idea for doubling the output. But when, eventually, an incentive scheme is worked out and No. 1 Bay are taking home £4 a week more, the majority in No. 2 Bay will probably decide to give the scheme a try and before long the old way of work will seem rather stupid to all of them.

The second principle is that where there has to be expropriation, there must be compensation. At times, undoubtedly, compensation may seem, and indeed be, unduly generous; but the alternative, expropriation without compensation, is both arbitrary and harsh. If the rich are thought to have too much, then they can all be taxed at a uniform rate according to their wealth. This is equitable. What is inequitable is that particular classes of assets, held by rich and poor alike, should be expropriated, while other assets escape. It will almost invariably be found that the rich man has scented the danger a long while before, and that the man holding the asset when the time comes is poor and poorly advised. When a man acquires property of any kind, he does so under the law of the land as it then stands. He has the right to remain in possession of it until he gives it up voluntarily, and in this reasonable expectation he arranges his way of life. The government may decide that the law as it stood was unjust to the community as a whole, that it hampered economic growth and that it ought to be changed. Nevertheless it must respect the consequences of its own previous attitude, and the changes should not be retrospective; property acquired under existing law should not be taken away again. This is the difference between change of government and revolution. The revolutionaries repudiate all previous obligations, while a new constitutional government will endorse whatever obligations were properly entered into by its predecessor. The Christian, believing that God's world is rational and orderly, must favour a rational and orderly form of government, governed by the rule of law and bringing some certainty and order into men's relations with one another.

While the Christian will not want to overturn existing property rights, he will be anxious to see that property is acquired in a fair and rational way, and that there is no aggregation of private wealth which would result in undue concentration of economic power. A system which taxes wealth on its transfer from one man to another is in accordance with this principle, even if by a progressive rate of tax it ensures the reduction of the great aggregations of private wealth.

There are some lesser, but important, principles for the Christian. The so-called 'welfare state' today ensures a certain standard of care for those unable to earn their own support. This would seem a vital Christian objective. The New Testament is full of injunctions to care for the 'widow and fatherless'. The economic system should provide an efficient safety net, which, as far as possible, protects everyone who might fall into need. The political argument today is not so much about the principle of the welfare state as about its application. Some feel that to protect the minority who are in want there is no need to have free medicine for all, and there is much argument about council house tenants who have higher incomes than those in private houses who support them through the rates. However, this is a matter of proper and equitable administration rather than a matter of Christian principle. It is perhaps worth mentioning, however, that the Christian cannot feel that his responsibilities are ended when he knows that those in need are financially provided for. The Christian still has responsibilities of a non-economic nature. Old people require company and time and patience, and other needs which cannot be met by writing out cheques.

Christians must qualify the desire for greater efficiency by the requirement that those who produce should be treated with dignity and consideration. Factory Acts and laws regulating hours of work must be regarded as a minimum. The Christian should work for higher standards for the health and protection of the worker and for those small but significant measures which give him standing in his own eyes and in the eyes of the community. There seems to be no reason why, in due course, the worker on the shop floor should not have the same standing as the office worker. Because we live in a competitive world, this cannot all be done overnight, but improvement in plant welfare should have its place when the surplus is divided between shareholder, state and worker.

How then do these principles fit in with the various economic systems at present current in the world? It will be clear that the crux of the matter is to reconcile the freedom and dignity which the Christian demands for the individual with his aims for the eradication of poverty. In the West we are inclined to think only of political freedom, but what kind of freedom can be enjoyed by the Indian peasant with an annual income of £25? By his poverty he is imprisoned in his village, in his social system, in his ignorance and, above all, in his inefficient means of production, which prevents even a hope of escape in the future. We should recognize that freedom to vote is not enough if it does not bring freedom from poverty in its train. Which of the major economic systems best reconciles the twin aims of political freedom and freedom from poverty?

Most Christians feel that communism, while it may aim at freedom from poverty, can hope to achieve this aim only at the cost of an intolerable loss of political freedom. So strong is this view that in most Protestant countries communism is not even a live political issue. It is true that communism can have local variations and might be modified if voluntarily adopted in a country with long traditions of political freedom, but there is much which appears to be of the essence of communism which a Christian cannot accept. It is avowedly atheistic and totalitarian, it regards material benefits as ends in themselves and allows all kinds of injustice to minorities in order to achieve its ends. Even laying aside these political objections, the communist economic system with its combination of state ownership and central economic control seems bound to weaken the freedom of the individual beyond the point which the Christian would consider tolerable. There are no strikes East of the Iron Curtain. For all these reasons, Christians who are free to choose have avoided the communist path, even though those who live in communist countries should obey their rulers in all matters which are not essential to their faith.

The countries where communism has gained support have been based, for the most part, on a static, semi-feûdal capitalism, which cared for the rich and powerful, but had little regard for the poor. There is all the difference in the world between these economic systems and the 'market economies' of Western Europe and North America, held in check by strong central government, effective social welfare and anti-trust laws. The Christian cannot support a system which does not have as a primary aim a substantial improvement in the lot of the ordinary man.

The economic systems in the Western world today represent various shades of opinion between capitalist 'market economies' and socialist 'planned economies'. The former emphasizes the freedom of the individual and the latter the social purposes of economic improvement. There is much that is good in the present compromise between socialism and capitalism, and there is much in the extremes in both systems which would, unsoftened by this compromise, be inimical to Christian ideals. At the one extreme, the wholesale nationalization of industry would seem to give far too great a concentration of power, and this would, sooner or later, detract from the dignity and independence of the individual. At the other extreme, it is fairly clear that the impersonal market mechanism must give way to, and be governed by, overriding social considerations. It should be our servant and not our master. It does seem, however, that we could do better than a compromise between two extreme positions and that it should be possible to evolve a more positive economic system from the principles which we have laid down. The next chapter tries to give some rough outlines of the kind of system which could both safeguard Christian principles and embody Christian ideals.

CHAPTER FOUR

THE SOCIAL RESPONSIBILITY OF BIG BUSINESS

Most Christians have become chary of the pronouncement of those churchmen and others who attempt to ally Christian teaching to their own particular political views. It sometimes seems that preachers have become politicians, and politicians preachers. For this reason, many Christians have been reluctant to give time and attention to the relation of their faith to social problems and have felt that their best contribution was personal piety and the simple proclamation of essential truth.

In the long run, persistence in this view would be a pity. It is necessary for every generation of Christians to make a conscious effort to disentangle the principles for which they stand from encrusted social attitudes and to restate those principles in their relation to new social forces. This is something very different from the attempts to mobilize the churches behind particular political campaigns or parties. The Church cannot subscribe to broad political platforms which include many issues on which it is not qualified to comment, but it must be in a position to advise its own members on matters of conduct when they find themselves in uncharted seas, subject to stresses and strains and conflicts of loyalty for which there is no apparent precedent in church teaching. A church which does not attempt to grapple with these new situations is in danger of encouraging its members to lead two different lives, one of traditional Christian morality in the family and the church, and another for weekdays when 'business is business', something the parson cannot hope to pronounce upon or even understand.

No-one has put this better than Professor Tawney:

> No change of system or machinery can avert those causes of social malaise which consist in the egotism, greed, or quarrelsomeness of human nature. What it can do is to create an environment in which those are not the qualities which are encouraged.
>
> During the last two centuries Europe, and particularly industrial Europe, has seen the development of a society in which what is called personal religion continues to be taught as the rule of individual conduct, but in which the very

conception of religion as the inspiration and standard of social life and corporate effort has been forgotten. Possessing no standards of their own, the churches were at the mercy of those who did possess them. They relieved the wounded and comforted the dying but they dared not enter the battle.

Christians are a sect, and a small sect, in a Pagan Society. But they can be a sincere sect. A good Pagan is not a Christian. The Church will not pretend that he is, or endeavour to make its own Faith acceptable to him by diluting the distinctive ethical attributes of Christianity till they become inoffensive, at the cost of becoming trivial. It need not seek to soften the materialism of principalities and powers with mild doses of piety administered in an apologetic whisper. It will teach as one having authority, and it will have sufficient confidence in its Faith to believe that it requires neither artificial protection nor judicious understatement in order that such truth as there is in it may prevail.

The evangelical emphasis on personal salvation has tended to the view that this is the sole purpose of the Church, and that apart from personal salvation little could be done for fallen humanity.

In dealing with the world outside the Church, the Christian must balance the doctrine of original sin with the doctrine of common grace. We are told that, despite the presence of evil, God is everywhere present in the world of His creation, upholding all His creatures in both being and activity (see, for instance, Acts 17:25, 28; Colossians 1:17; Hebrews 1: 3). Some divine influence is granted to all men, and man is restrained from the worst effects of sin while this world lasts. Only in exceptional cases does God withdraw the restraint completely and 'give them over to a reprobate mind', allowing sin to work out its full destructive consequences here on earth. The Church is the instrument of saving grace, but both Church and state are instruments of common grace, and the responsibility of the Christian in either is not limited to the work of conversion. The Church has a duty, not only to preach the gospel, but also to preach the moral law. Individual Christians who are in a position to influence the standards of society must try to indicate as best they may how the standards of the moral law should affect the issues of the day. This has seldom been as important as it is now, when standards of behaviour are lower in Britain than they have been for a long time and when most of the professing Church seems intent of having no standards of its own. The Christian should not over-estimate the power of common grace. It will not make a man regenerate. But neither should he under-estimate it. 'Thy will be done in earth, as it is in heaven' is a prayer we are commanded to make, and it would be lack of faith to wonder whether God has the means to answer it.

Part of our difficulty arises from the different teachings on the relation of Church and state. The Erastian view is that the Church is dependent on the state and the Roman Catholic view that the state is dependent on the Church. The view of the majority of Protestants today is that Church and state are essentially different and rightfully independent. Both owe their origin to God, but were instituted for different objects, the state for promoting and securing the outward order and good of human society, the Church to advance its spiritual well-being. Their powers are different. The state has powers of coercion. It 'beareth not the sword in vain'. The Church can use instruction, reproof, censure and excommunication, but when these means have been used, its powers are exhausted. Finally and perhaps most important for our purpose, the administrations are different. The hierarchy of the Church has no authority in matters of state, and the rulers of the state have no authority in the affairs of the Church. Where a matter is unmistakably spiritual, the Church has a right to speak with authority; where the matter is political, she has no right to speak in her capacity as a Church.

This does not mean that the voice of Christians should not be heard in political matters or that they should not influence legislation. What it does mean is that they should enter the arena as citizens and stand or fall on their own merits without calling in aid the authority and reputation of the Church. There has been a long tradition in Britain of statesmen who have professed the Christian faith, have put forward political policies based on what they conceived as being Christian principles and have appealed for support to the consciences of individual Christians. The best known are Wilberforce and Shaftesbury, but the line must include many of those who promoted the great Reform Bill of 1832, and runs from Pym, Hampden and Cromwell to Gladstone and, in our own day, such dissimilar characters as Stafford Cripps and Quintin Hogg. One does not have to agree with all their views or vouch for their doctrinal purity to make the limited point that they acted in this tradition, that they tried to apply what they conceived to be Christian teaching to political policy wherever they thought it relevant.

When we come to tackle particular issues, we realize that the Church is wise to avoid squandering its collective authority by 'ex cathedra' pronouncements on this problem and that. Any practical application of Christian principles must take into account a whole host of technical details. There is no point in coming to a conclusion which may be perfect academically but unattainable in practice. It was not enough to be in favour of the general principle of the abolition of rotten boroughs.

The ideas had to be clothed in a series of detailed and practical proposals. If universal suffrage was not immediately practicable, then where was the line to be drawn? If the ignorance of the workers was argued against it, then how should the workers be educated?

But as soon as we get down to details, a whole series of alternatives opens up. Two groups of equally sound and earnest Christians might, because they had slightly different backgrounds, information and experience, come to quite different conclusions. One might well be right and the other wrong, but the outsider would not necessarily see this. A later generation tackling the same problem would almost certainly modify the original proposals in the light of experience. It would be quite wrong for a Church which taught eternal truth to be identified with any particular dogma in the shifting world of political ideas. But it is both right and desirable that groups of Christians should be continuously engaged in the task of working out methods of incorporating the eternal ideals of their faith in practical proposals to meet the changing needs of daily life.

This may seem to be a rather lengthy preamble to justify our right to come out with some positive proposals about the place of the joint stock company in national life, but there have been long gaps in the tradition and it is as well to state the basis, scope and limitations of the proposals we make.

Business, in the sense of the small family business, is, of course, nothing new to the Church. It is universal and age-old, and its particular temptations are understood and dealt with specifically in the Bible itself, which teaches, for instance, that to give short measure is wrong and to withhold wages is wrong (see, e.g., Deuteronomy 25:15; Micah 6:11; Leviticus 19:13; Jeremiah 22:13; James 5: 4). The world of small business is not fundamentally different in our day, and although it has its problems, it is not the immediate purpose of this chapter to deal with them. The new forces are big business, the active and extensive direction of economic life by strong central governments and – in certain countries – the power of organized labour. These new economic forces are more powerful than the world has ever seen, and advances have been made which previously seemed impossible. In every corner of the globe people who have lived just above starvation level have had their expectations raised and demand a better life. Age-old traditions have been put under strain on a universal scale, as the prospect of high industrial wages has taken labour away from feudal estates and family small-holdings. Individual Christians are involved in these changes as pastors, missionaries, teachers and parents, but above all they are involved when they are part of the economic machine itself. They do not as 'organization men' escape from their responsibility as Christians.

In the last chapter we came to the conclusion that neither communism nor feudalism were economic systems which could command support, though the Christian must agree with the objective of raising the living standards of the poor which the communists profess. We also felt that the extreme positions of capitalism and socialism were not compatible with the welfare, dignity and freedom of the individual, but that the modifications each had imposed on the other had produced a compromise which was more acceptable, if not ideal. We felt that it should be possible, however, to construct a legislative framework for our means of production which embodied Christian ideals more directly. In contrast to capitalism, where the residual benefit went to the owner, it should be explicitly aimed at the increase of the wealth of the community at large. In contrast to state ownership, it should reserve to the state only what required to be reserved by the strict criterion of public interest, and should aim for the freedom of the individual in choice of job and choice of expenditure. It should not replace the power of big business by the power of bureaucracy, but aim to limit the powers of both to what was functionally necessary for economic growth, and aim to make these necessary powers more specifically responsible to society. Above all, these aims must be realizable in practice and should, therefore, be fulfilled by adapting the existing system rather than uprooting it.

Many may feel that the existing modifications of capitalism are sufficient and that there is no need to go further. Capitalism today is hardly recognizable as being in the same species as the *laissez-faire* capitalism of the nineteenth century. Big business is accountable to its shareholders and lenders under company law. It is accountable to its employees under social legislation governing factory conditions, hours of employment, method of payment, right to unionize and right to strike. It is accountable to its customers under the laws of contract, the laws governing the description and sale of goods and, more recently, by legislation under the restrictive trades practices acts, which in America are very strictly policed and enforced. Its power is limited by acts against monopoly and by high taxation of both corporations and individuals. No-one, least of all company directors, could be blamed for the feeling that 'enough is enough'.

It is only when we look more closely that we see the gaps in the present structure, the weakness of the concepts of social responsibility and the relative ineffectiveness of such legislation as there now is to embody them. Whatever the theoretical power of the shareholder, it is now generally recognized that it is almost impossible for shareholders to call to account the actions of directors of big businesses with widespread share ownership. The board of a large public company is, in practice, a self-perpetuating body. Almost all additions are made by nomination of the directors. The majority of public companies have boards composed largely or wholly of executive directors, and their interests as executives and their interests as directors may not always coincide, particularly when it comes to commenting to the owners on their performance as executives. As a result, these enormous centres of economic power, containing most of the nation's productive resources and the practical outlet for its inventiveness, are in the effective control of self-perpetuating bodies. The best public companies are well aware of the dangers of inbreeding. They recruit to the board strictly on merit and bring in active, able and independent men from outside. But for every company which does this, there must be half a dozen where power is effectively retained by two or three men whose ideas and objectives can only be challenged by the long drawn out pressure of events. This is not the best formula for maximization of profits, let alone for economic growth and a rising standard of living. The answer of capitalism is the 'take-over bid', and the threat of this has no doubt done some good; but this is at best a blunt instrument and at worst disruptive if not destructive.

The disappearance of shareholder control is not a plot by established business tycoons. It is the result of a combination of the competitive framework within which business operates and widespread public shareholding. If business is to compete, it must be allowed to keep private a large measure of information on its position and performance, and this information cannot be kept private if it is given to thousands of shareholders whose interests are not limited to that particular company. Even if more information is given than at present, this basic contradiction cannot be resolved within the present framework.

What is true for the shareholder is also true for the employee and his representatives. Their information on the costs, competitive position and potential productivity of the company is strictly limited by the degree of secrecy necessary to the competitive system. It is difficult to believe that the settlement of wage negotiations is at the same advanced level as legislation on working conditions. The union leader does not have the information to enable him to point out in detail the methods by which management might recover wage increases by higher productivity. A weak management in non-competitive conditions will pass the increase on by raising prices. Otherwise, the bargaining degenerates into threat and bluff instead of being, as it should, a constructive negotiation between informed men seeking a reconciliation of their respective interests.

As a by-product of this situation, power on the union side has tended to shift from the responsible union leaders to the activists, because when it comes to threat and bluff, the activists are usually more successful. It has been argued that the unions need to reform their leadership. No doubt many unions do not pay their leaders enough and do not obtain the calibre of leadership they should, but the question still remains as to what the unions can do with this calibre of leadership when they have it. Unless they have access to more useful information than is publicly available at the moment, it is hard to see how they can bring constructive pressure to bear on management for improvement in productivity. But efficient and informed union leaders could do much to level up industrial pro-ductivity and compel backward management to adopt methods and machinery which would give greater revenue per worker. This should do much to restore the authority of the legitimate union leaders and to cut the unofficial activists down to size.

Despite its disadvantages, competitive capitalism has advantages. In classic economic theory it is the method of protecting the customer. Theoretically it should enable the efficient firms to be the pace-setters and to attract custom, brains and capital away from the firms which are less efficient. It should reward the successful innovator and encourage enterprise. It gives freedom to move from one job to another. It tends to minimize the national effects of mistakes in judgment which any single group of men are bound to make. It is small wonder that to so many lovers of freedom the market economy seems both right and efficient and not to be tampered with. But those who have to operate it do not always see it quite so idealistically. It is at its best in small industries with low capital investment and easily comparable products. But in large and highly capitalized industries, it is almost essential to have some form of price discipline, and pricing methods appropriate to the disposal of surplus stocks of toffee-apples are not appropriate to the pricing of electricity or computers. It is also open to purely speculative disturbance. The official attitude hovers between a belief that competition is a good thing and the knowledge that strict enforcement could, in some cases, have the most destructive results. The American answer lies in massive anti-trust legislation. But legislation is a ponderous and inflexible instrument to meet a complex and changing situation, and no other country has moved so far in this direction. There should certainly be legislation against both restrictive trade practices and against monopolies, and British monopoly legislation should be more effective, but a more precise and more flexible instrument is necessary to look after the public interest.

Left to itself, competition has some less beneficial side effects. Where action is in the public interest, but expensive, it is less than likely that a company which is fighting for its place in the market will feel free to accept a burden which its competitors do not have to share. Who will fill their plants with low-priced export orders and leave competition free to take a larger share of the home market? Who will take on the burden of training and re-training to have its newly-trained men poached by competitors who have not carried the burden? Who can maintain quality when an efficient competitor cuts it? Competitive advertising expenditure must be matched, however excessive its scale. Large capital expenditure schemes of competing companies in the same industry tend to hold back and go forward together to protect each company's market share, whereas the public interest would seem to demand that they be co-ordinated and phased to avoid swings between too little capacity and too much. There seems, therefore, to be an area, too large to be comfortable, in which the market economy does not automatically look after the public interest.

It must also be admitted that, in the market economy, competition does not have the quick and beneficial effects which economic theory would lead us to expect. Efficient companies do not reduce their prices and put the inefficient companies into liquidation. Movement of capital, labour and competition from inefficient to efficient is sluggish at best. Ingrained habits keep staff, labour and customers where they are long after it would pay them to move. But, in any case, our physical, and above all our human, investment in great enterprises can hardly allow us to agree that the best solution is to stand by while one or other of them in charge of encrusted and immovable management goes slowly downhill under the pressure of blind market forces towards the final break up and redundancy. If our competition is to be more than half-hearted, we must feel that those who come under pressure will be made to put things right before it is too late.

These problems have been examined time and again, but very few viable solutions have been put forward. It is easy enough to see what is wrong, and we have had some brilliant analyses, all of which have faltered and fumbled before a solution. This is partly because the major political parties have seemed committed to doctrinaire solutions, but largely because of the comparative novelty of big business as an institution and lack of understanding of the way in which it works. Most of the analysts have been academic economists or journalists. Few practising industrialists have had time or inclination to think out solutions. This, combined with our dependence on big·business, makes responsible politicians reluctant to do anything which might interfere with its successful working. This situation is changing. Understanding of the complex affairs of industry is increasing together with an awareness that economic growth is a proper objective. Both major political parties are becoming less attached to dogma and are looking for a solution which will best combine freedom and economic growth.

British law has already accepted extensive limitations on the rights of private ownership where these go beyond personal needs, and while Christian teaching requires respect for personal property, these limitations would be agreeable to Christian teaching on the respect we must have for our neighbours. Limitation on the rights of property are particularly appropriate in the case of major economic units which are large enough individually to affect the life of the community. These should be directed in the public interest as well as in the interests of private owners. It may not always be easy to define the public interest, but this is no reason for not making the attempt. From time to time as conditions change it should be as precisely defined as possible, so that action in the public interest is not arbitrary, unpredictable or unequal between companies in the areas defined as being of public interest. Major companies should be accountable for their actions and policies. For instance, it might be decided that policies of companies employing more than so many people or worth more than so many million pounds should be accountable for their policies on exports, the amount, timing and location of investment, redundancy, training, research, wages and dividends. This would enable the government to understand the operations of those companies controlling the 'commanding heights of the economy'. They could then define the public interest and isolate the areas in which, without direction, public interest and competitive capitalism might be at variance. This would enable them to give advice, promote joint action in industry and take such legislative and fiscal measures as were necessary. It could care for the public interest without the dangers to variety, competition and personal freedom which it would incur if it assumed direct control of industrial life. This combination of freedom and accountability would seem to answer Christian principles best.

It is not enough to put these ideas forward. They have to be clothed in a workable organizational structure. The gap between government and individual companies is too great to implement these policies without organizational change. The National Economic Development Council goes a little way but not far enough. There can be little effective reconciliation of private and public interest without breaking the problems down into sections which have some common denominators. One way of doing this is the creation of bodies of similar composition to NEDC for each major industry. Their jobs would be to understand the affairs of the industry, identify areas, such as those mentioned above, where the public interest was involved and to agree with the companies' methods of dealing with these matters of public interest.

It now seems certain that this will, in fact, be the pattern of the future in Britain. Early in 1963 the Labour party executive decided that its policy would be to form Industrial Planning Councils to consist of trade unions and employers' representatives and independents (including academics), together with representatives of the government departments concerned. Each Council would have its own small permanent staff. They would rely on the powers of information and persuasion with the ultimate sanctions of publicity and recommendation to government for legislative action. They would cover investment (including location of industry), exports, manpower (including training), and industrial efficiency.

The National Economic Development Council, under the chairmanship of the Conservative Chancellor, in November, 1963 formally approved arrangements to set up Economic Development Committees. Their terms of reference are: 1. To examine the economic performance, prospects and plans of their particular industry, and to assess periodically its progress in relation to the national growth objectives; and 2. To consider ways of improving the industry's economic performance, competitive power and efficiency, and to draw up reports and recommendations on those matters as appropriate. Each Committee will have about fifteen members – ten representing management and unions; one spokesman for the NEDC office and another from the government department covering the industry; with one or two independents and a chairman.

When the Labour Government was returned to power in October 1964, it confirmed that it would use the Economic Development Committees. It retained the terms of reference and expanded the number of committees to cover the greater part of industrial and commercial employment.

In the meantime the competitive system limits the extent to which any one company can get out of line in the exercise of social responsibility, but not all socially desirable policies require money. Others which do require money are not so expensive as to make a company uncompetitive, particularly if its management are just that little bit more conscientious and efficient. Higher morale gives lower staff and labour turnover and a cooperative attitude oils the wheels in innumerable ways. Managers do not have to wait for the ideal world to begin to exercise social responsibility. Shareholders can and should be interested in more than their dividend and should express their views whenever they have the chance. Their money should be, as we suggest in a later chapter, invested in companies which seem to serve a useful social purpose and which exercise a positive social responsibility to customers, workers and to the community. But though there may be direct benefits from the exercise of social responsibility, the Christian must always act on his principles whether in material terms he gains or loses.

CHAPTER FIVE

THE SOCIAL RESPONSIBILITY OF TRADES UNIONS

FROM time to time we read in the papers that a Christian has refused, on conscientious grounds, to join a union and that pressure has been put on his employer to dismiss him. It would be unnatural not to sympathize with a fellow Christian standing alone on a point of principle against the joint might of union and employer. But, whatever our emotions, we must each examine for ourselves the principles involved. What is the Christian's view of trade unions, of union membership and of strike action?

The conscientious argument against joining a union is usually based on the injunction, 'Be ye not unequally yoked together with unbelievers'. The union is, it is said, a body largely composed of non-Christians and the Christian, therefore, has no right to be associated with it. The logic of this case demands, of course, that we should not be associated with any other non-Christian body, and some exponents of this view also condemn membership of universities and of professional bodies, not to mention political parties. The Christian is thus cut off from the main stream of secular life around him. It is hard to reconcile this interpretation of the 'unequal yoke' with the general tone of the New Testament doctrine, especially passages such as Romans 13. It is much more likely that the 'unequal yoke' refers to a more intimate relationship such as marriage; yet even in marriage where one partner is subsequently converted, Paul tells them that they are not obliged to leave the unbelieving husband or the unbelieving wife. But even when the argument of the unequal yoke is excluded, there are still some who are uneasy, or at least far from enthusiastic, about trades union membership, and it is necessary to examine the pros and cons.

Is a trade union in itself an association worthy of a Christian's support and membership? It is perhaps significant that those countries with the strongest Christian tradition have also the strongest trade union tradition. We do not hear of trade disputes east of the Iron Curtain. The Christian faith teaches us respect for the individual, and if society respects the individual he must be protected from the possibility of exploitation by those who employ him. He can and should be protected by law, but law is not sufficiently flexible or versatile to meet the kind of situations which arise on the shop floor. The law can operate only in black and white situations. It can be enforceable against the employer only where there is some firm yardstick by which his actions can be measured. Minimum wages, number of persons in a given working area, fencing of dangerous machinery, employment of children are all measurable and are, therefore, amenable to legislation. But skill differentials, annual wage awards, general working conditions are relative matters and the arguments both ways become too complex for legislation. They are issues for negotiation if they are not to become issues of conflict. But the wage-earner is in no position to negotiate as an individual. If he tried, the negotiation would be hopelessly one-sided. His strength must lie in uniting with his fellows so that he negotiates on level terms. Nor is this enough unless he is able to exercise some means of enforcing his point of view, should persuasion fail. It is commonly agreed that the best way of doing this is the collective withdrawal of labour.

The really effective protection is the right of association combined with the right collectively to withdraw labour. In Britain these rights are thought to be sufficiently important to have the protection of the law. It is true that if all employers lived up to Christian ideals there might well be no need for unions. But in this imperfect world the employer is no better and no worse than the next man. If we are to be realistic we must certainly agree that trades unions perform a useful and necessary function. No better machinery has been found to protect the individual in our society as it is organized, and potentially at least they are capable of much constructive work. To say that unions are necessary is not, of course, to say that every union is perfect or that the conduct of unionists is always wise and unselfish. Employers find that, as a rule, fair dealing with unions makes for a reasonable response, but there are well-known and much publicized exceptions even to this rule. This itself should not deter the Christian either from joining a union or from dealing with one. If the Christian lives up to his own ideals, nothing but good can come from the encounter. Most unions have a democratic constitution, and if members do not bother to vote, this is hardly the fault of the institution. Indeed much industrial conflict would be avoided if employers and employees made proper use of the union machinery.

If these arguments are accepted the Christian should have a positive attitude to trades unions. They should have the Christian's general support. He should not simply accept them grudgingly as a necessary evil.

This goes not only for the Christian who is eligible to join a union but for the Christian manager and employer. Comment and criticism on the affairs of the union should be constructive and aimed to help them to look after the interests of their members, and should not be aimed at undermining or damaging their position. The Christian must support an orderly society and he should, therefore, support those bodies which are concerned with resolving men's disputes with each other in an orderly way. In a number of well-known cases industrial anarchy within a particular company can be traced back to an original refusal by management to deal with responsible unions. This may have been done with the highest of intentions by a paternalistic management sure that it would always do its best for the men. But as a result power on the labour side has either been taken over by irresponsible, self-appointed leaders or, without any clear guidance from management, a dozen or more separate unions have been fighting for the men's allegiance, have established themselves in separate parts of the plant and the whole bargaining process has become thoroughly disorganized.

One feels compelled to say this because there is still much basic hostility to the unions, particularly among those who are somewhat remote from the industrial scene. To quote the Political and Economic Planning pamphlet *Trade Unions in a Changing Society*, 'Sickness and accidents, for example, in terms of time lost are nearly hundredfold more important than strikes yet they receive perhaps less than one per cent of the public attention.' The pamphlet's explanation is that some press comment is unbalanced and, at root, hostile to trade unionism. Attention is almost wholly devoted to the failings of the unions, and little awareness is shown of their present contribution and their future contribution to industrial relations. The result is to increase the defensiveness of the unions' attitudes, to sharpen their sense of apartness, to give ammunition to those elements in the union movement who wish to prolong the class struggle and to make all unionists instinctively suspicious of the basic motives behind advice offered to them from the outside.

Even allowing for a hostile press, there is a genuine feeling that since the war union power has become excessive, and that it has been used to advance the interests of trade unionists at the expense of the rest of the country. Certainly, during the last decade, real wages (after deducting the inflationary element) have gone up by a third and many of those who are not unionized have had no corresponding benefits. Certainly, too, some prominent union leaders have thrown their weight around in public, and none of us like to see the growth of private positions of power.

Union power is not, in fact, as monolithic as it appears. In the United Kingdom there are about 10 million union members out of 22 million employees. As manual work has declined in importance so has the position of the union in certain key industries. In the ten years to 1958 the total numbers of employees in manufacturing increased by 900,000, and of this increase only 300,000 were operatives, the remaining 600,000 being administrative, clerical and technical staff. The proportion of staff and technicians employed in manufacturing increased from 16 per cent to 21 per cent.

In Britain only one non-manual worker in five is a union member, and non-manual membership is heavily concentrated in public employment, notably the civil service, local government and the railways. Union membership is high in coal mining (90 per cent), railways (85 per cent) and local and national government (84 per cent and 81 per cent), but is very much lower in industry generally outside the nationalized industries and government. In engineering, for instance, the union membership was only 51 per cent in 1958. In agriculture it was 26 per cent, and in distribution 15 per cent. There certainly seems to be no direct relation between those activities which are highly unionized and those activities where wages have gone ahead particularly rapidly.

If the extent of union power is not so wide as sometimes appears, there is no point in denying that unions do have power and do exercise it, and that anyone interested, as the Christian is, in the dignity and liberty of the individual has a right to examine the facts of this power and the way in which it is exercised.

The right to form trade unions and the right to withhold labour normally go together, because the right to withhold labour is usually the only sanction available to the working man. It is a principle of British justice that the courts will not force one man to work for another, and this principle is at one with the Christian principle of respect for the dignity of the individual. But the right to withhold labour is usually only effective if it is exercised collectively. Any breach of collective action by a minority damages the sanction. If some do not accept the authority of their elected leaders, those who do are placed in a very difficult position. Their action may be made ineffective and they have, by loyalty to their leaders, marked themselves as less cooperative than those who did not strike. There is strong pressure on the weaker strikers to return. The negotiating strength of the union, which is based on its ability to command the support of members, is bound to be weakened.

It is sometimes hard for professional people, who negotiate their own terms of work and whose job demands individual judgment and initiative, to see the need for the worker to accept collective discipline. His sympathy naturally tends to be with the independently-minded worker who is prepared to stand up to the union leadership. But those who take this line usually picture the union calling the men out. Today we are far more likely to find that the man who does not accept union discipline is the extremist and that the union official is counselling moderation. Union authority is indivisible. The authority which calls a man out is the same as the authority which calls him back. If a responsible elected authority is undermined, an irresponsible self-appointed authority is as likely as not to step into the void.

Unfortunately there is a decided increase in the number of unconstitutional strikes. These were estimated in a statement by the Minister of Labour on 14 February, 1963 as running at around 2,000 a year and causing upwards of 90 per cent of disputes in Britain. However, the impact of strikes is usually over-estimated. In 1962 over a third were for less than a day and only $12\frac{1}{2}$ per cent lasted longer than six days. In the twelve years to 1961 only 235 days were lost per thousand employees over key industries in Britain as against 1,343 days in the USA. (The actual number of strikes is not an entirely reliable indicator, since there is no way of measuring the concessions made by management to buy off a strike.)

Although the power of the unions is less than is generally credited to them, and is perhaps more spectacular than real, they do exercise power, and have instruments of power which in particular cases certainly seem to be a threat to individual liberty. Of these the most controversial is probably the 'closed shop'. This is a factory where membership of a particular union is a condition of employment. It must be said at once that many employers are in favour of the closed shop, and far prefer to deal with one union which is in an effective position to negotiate than with a series of quite different unions. It avoids demarcation disputes between unions, and it avoids the whole factory being closed down because of a dispute in a particular section. There can also be a closed shop in a limited part of a factory, and although this does not have all the benefits of one union answering for one factory, it still has limited benefits for both sides. If the man joins a factory where there is a closed shop as a condition of employment and he accepts this condition, he can hardly complain about it afterwards. The difficulty arises where a union has a large percentage of the shop in membership and does not see why the minority should obtain benefits without joining. It then demands a closed shop, and if any employees stand out the management is faced with the alternative of a costly strike or the dismissal of employees, who may be long-service employees, about something which has nothing to do with their competence in their job.

The unions say that the desire for the closed shop has often arisen as a reaction against the use by the employers of the open shop to break strikes. In other cases, it has arisen from a pride in craft skill. In yet others, it has arisen through disruption by the minority to the damage of the majority. Ernest Bevin, for instance, tried to get a closed shop in London Transport because of the disruption being caused by a small union being led by the communists. But perhaps the most general reason is the feeling on the part of the union that there is no point in setting up to negotiate with the employer if you cannot enforce your own side of the agreement.

Recognition and the ability to enforce agreements are the twin pillars on which a union stands and without which it cannot function. In looking at the closed shop the question the union has to ask is, 'Is our bargaining strength enough?' In the experience of most unionists those who did not join were seldom, if ever, acting for the principles of individual liberty. Only the tiny minority of those who had religious scruples were doing anything more than trying to avoid collective obligations. The unions say that since they are voluntary societies they have to have some sanction over their members if they are going to achieve anything for them. The only real sanction of a voluntary society is expulsion, but if expulsion makes no difference to a man (or to a member union of the TUC), then it is no sanction. In an open shop expulsion makes little difference, but in a closed shop it does. It is, of course, true that the taking away of a union ticket in a closed craft union is a considerable power to give to union officials, and it must be exercised fairly. In case of abuse the individual is protected by law, and this is an area in which the law can operate. Many unions have a 'natural justice' rule, but these are no longer necessary since the courts will imply the rule even if it is not in the constitution.

The TUC has usually advised its members not to enforce a closed shop unless they feel it to be absolutely necessary. They take the view that it is hardly ever necessary now to enforce a closed shop to obtain recognition. If half a dozen long-service employees stand out it is usually an unnecessary imposition to require their conformity or dismissal. Organization is a means to an end and not an end in itself. On the other hand, if those outside the union endanger the livelihood of their workmates, they are in the same position as the man who runs a machine dangerously and action has to be taken to protect those who work with him. The union view would be that the employer was perfectly entitled to disagree with their diagnosis and to act accordingly provided he was prepared to settle the dispute in the normal way. The unions point out that there is a limit to the number of people they would wish to recruit to the unions on this principle and it is not part of their job, they say, to extend their activities to cover those jobs whose occupants are sufficiently distinctive to deal with employers individually and make their own bargain for employment. There is only a need to unionize if the unions do for a man something he cannot do so well for himself. Though there will be times when a union feels that it must have a closed shop, it does not seem to be an inevitable part of trade union activity.

The major instrument of union power is the withdrawal of labour. Just as the closed shop is the union's sanction against its own members, the strike is its sanction against the employer. Even if the Christian agrees that this sanction has been found historically necessary he may still feel some repugnance at the idea of putting the public to inconvenience or hardship in order to enforce his sectional interests. Even if he feels bound in the end to go along with the majority, he may feel that there should be some Christian standard by which he could decide when a strike was justified and when it was not. As soon as you go into it, however, it quickly appears that it is a very difficult matter on which to lay down general principles.

Strike action often arises as much from a lack of confidence in the other side as from immediate and tangible issues. Two different managements could make exactly the same proposals to their respective union opposite numbers. In the one case the union might accept, in the knowledge that the management were traditionally fair and that this was an honest attempt to make the best possible offer. In the other case, the offer might equally correctly be interpreted to be yet one more attempt by management to backtrack on an existing understanding which, if accepted by the union, would undermine months or years of patient negotiation. They might feel that in these circumstances a strike was their only method of bringing home to management the folly of prevarication.

Some union leaders allow themselves to be guided by the general principle that they will strike only where they are sure of a broad measure of public sympathy for their case. This is not an infallible rule because the public may be misled, or the matter may be so detailed and intimate to the particular plant that the public could not conceivably judge the issues; but it does, at any rate, take into account some independent judgment of the situation. Reference by both sides to an independent tribunal is perhaps the safeguard against unnecessary strikes, provided both sides are prepared to be bound by the tribunal's judgment. Arbitration procedure now covers a very wide range of union activities. It is not infallible, arbitrators are themselves human, and it is thought by some that it has some inherent defects, but it is very much better than open and irreconcilable conflicts. It is natural and right for a Christian to deplore the use of force to settle a disagreement. The Christian regards patience as a virtue, and he should never be exasperated or stampeded into ill-considered action. He should try all other means before allowing a trial of strength, and should always do his best to promote ways and means for rational settlement of disputes. That is not to say he should be weak, but he should use his strength wisely. In industrial affairs, as in war, wise negotiators try, by convincing the other side of their good intentions, to avoid wasting the resources of both sides in an unnecessary build-up of fighting strength.

It is not unnatural to ask whether, if it is logical to bind employers by company law, there is any good reason why employees and their unions should not be similarly bound. There is, however, a very real difference between legislation limiting men in their dealings with other men's property and legislation governing the individual's personal liberty to work where he pleases and when he pleases. It is part of our belief in the dignity of the individual that the law in Britain will not enforce 'specific performance' of contracts of personal service—that is, it will not issue an order demanding that you actually perform a contract of service, it will only award damages for breach. As part of this principle, the government will not make a strike a criminal offence. Without departing from this principle, it is hard to make a man's right to work or refrain from working amenable to legislation. If it is desirable to have restrictions there must be some balancing factor, the removal or adjustment of which provides an extra-legal sanction. If the government can give something of real benefit to the union then, as a *quid pro quo*, the union could probably hold their members to reasonable restrictions. For instance, there is a current idea that the government should commit itself to a generous rate of economic growth provided the unions keep pay claims within a certain over-all limit. This has certain inherent defects and perhaps is too general and ambitious to be entirely practical. But though this sort of thing cannot be done all at once, if it were done effectively in a particular area and were successful, the union leaders would be enabled to obtain more general acceptance of this kind of bargain. Once this acceptance became wide-spread, they would then be able to apply pressure at the edges to obtain general acceptance throughout the movement. But before pressure could be applied successfully most people in the unions would have to believe that the particular proposition was a 'fair do'.

There are other minor objections to the imposition of legal obligations on the unions. The unions point out that companies who have to comply with the provisions of the Companies Act have full-time officers. Trade unions at the same level have to rely on part-time officers, many of whom will not have had any training for this kind of job. There would, therefore, be considerable technical difficulties in carrying out detailed obligations imposed by law. Nor are the unions anxious to have the kind of legislation on election and voting which would encourage union elections to become like parliamentary elections. They feel that the unions are concerned with mundane bread-and-butter affairs which do not and should not encourage high polls. High polls arise only by bringing in extraneous issues which have nothing to do with the union's true function and which would only cause disruption to their proper job. They regard communism, as such, as an extraneous issue which has nothing to do with the work of the unions, and senior people in the trade union movement feel that it is, therefore, a mistake for other groups (for instance, a religious group, such as the Catholics) to try to organize against them. They feel that this is a campaign on the communists' own ground. They do not want to see the day on which the union has 80 per cent poll because that would involve a public campaign and that, in turn, would almost certainly bring in issues external to union affairs. Therefore, they do not want the kind of legislation which would encourage high polls.

In Australia a very complete labour act was passed in 1952 which set out to reduce what are called 'irritation' strikes. It is interesting that there were 1,276 such strikes in 1950, yet two years after the act was passed, the number was 1,490. One understands that this trend has continued and that the act has failed to fulfil the hopes of those who drew it up. One is told that if the men think they have a grievance and believe that their only way to express it is by means of a strike, they carry on in defiance of all authority. In America the Taft/Hartley Act was passed in 1947 and is aimed to limit several union practices which are considered unfair. But the American record for strikes is, as we have seen, much worse than that in this country. There is, therefore, no hard evidence yet that more legal control of trade unions would help to improve their internal working or lessen the chance of industrial conflict.

Many people feel that one particular reform which would avoid control by minorities and ensure internal accountability is the requirement that all union decisions, particularly elections, should be by secret ballot. One gathers that the unions have no inherent objection to the use of secret ballots and, above a certain level, election to union offices are normally only by secret ballot. What they fear is that, if every member has the right to a ballot paper, a member who did not get one could bring an injunction at law which would halt the whole procedure, and since union records are usually kept by part-time officials and are not always guaranteed to be precisely complete, this might well bring the affairs of the unions to a grinding halt. If the rules allowed more latitude, ballots would still be open to twisting since the degree of supervision could hardly be the same as for local and national elections; there has in fact been one notorious case of ballot-rigging in the last few years. Ballots in unions come under the same general objection as referenda in parliamentary government. The best way may well be to give the officers of the union sufficient powers to make the decisions themselves without reference back. One of the reasons for suggesting ballots is their use as a means of controlling unofficial strikes. But the unions feel that the most practical way to do this is to delegate sufficient power from the unions to the local officers, and there seems to be something in this point.

Union ideology is very different from middle-class professional ideology. When a man joins a union he gives up his individual position in order to gain the protection and benefit of a collective position. He is not interested in competition at the expense of his mates. The essence of unionism is that you do not compete, you combine. Nor is he interested in the threat of international competition. He is inclined to the view that if you really want to be competitive, all you have to do is to live on rice. The union leaders say that manual workers do not just want more money. The aim of a union is to achieve for them something broader, and that is a better life. This might mean the opportunity to develop their personality outside the strict confines of a prosaic job. This could be achieved by shortening the working week or by an extension of the paid holiday.

This is quite different from the professional man's aim to develop himself through his work. The professional aims to a far greater extent to assimilate his work into his life. This may seem to many to be much more in accord with the Christian's view of work as a calling. It would seem to the Christian much better for unions and managements to try to upgrade the work force from semi-skilled to skilled work, as it has been upgraded from unskilled to semi-skilled, and to give men more responsibility and a bigger interest and personal stake in their job. It would seem desirable to make the work itself more dignified and worth while. But the union view would seem to be that the present balance between skilled and unskilled was what they had to deal with and will have to deal with in the foreseeable future. A massive shift from routine work would be a visionary and somewhat unreal objective at present. Nor do they say that men find routine work degrading. It enables them to occupy their minds with other things. What makes their work tolerable is its predictable rhythm, and it only becomes intolerable if this is upset by hectic or spasmodic pressure. It is very difficult to bridge this gulf in attitude to work and perhaps too easy for a professional to feel that his view is the Christian view. Nevertheless, although it may seem wrong to take an extreme view and regard our work as a drudgery, merely something to be got through with the minimum of trouble while our mind is elsewhere, there must be many Christians who cannot foresee a time when they will not have a dull job and who do find an outlet in their interests in the home, the community and Christian work.

The unions are not perfect and there is much that they could do to reform themselves, both in order to do their job more effectively and to police their own activities at shop-floor level. An industrialist hesitates to tell the other side its job – and the idea that there are never two sides nor any conflicting interests is nothing but a confusing myth – but it seems to be generally acknowledged that most union constitutions could be adapted to give greater flexibility in meeting new patterns of industry and employment and, in particular, in bringing local shop-floor bargaining back under union control; that they should find a way to raise their dues so that they can pay their officers a more reasonable salary and attract and train able officers for the future; and that they should find means of settling inter-union disputes so that these do not cause hardship to those not involved. These are all domestic matters well within their province, and for a Christian who felt the call to this kind of work there would seem to be a wide field of opportunity.

But the first task of those in management is to make constructive suggestions about their own actions and attitudes, and if managers also aim to be leaders, one cannot help feeling that the initiative in good labour relations should be with them. There is a good deal of truth in the old saying, 'There are no bad soldiers, only bad officers.' In a broadcast talk, published in *The Listener*, W. E. J. McCarthy, Research Fellow in Industrial Relations at Nuffield College, Oxford, says, 'Some pits are more strike-prone than others; some docks are peaceful; certain motor-car firms hardly ever have a strike. If one is to provide more than a very general and superficial explanation of strikes, one has to go beyond industrial generalities and ask why it is that in firm A, or in workshop B problems, solved elsewhere, result in strikes.' He investigated two coal mines near together, with similar conditions but very different strike records. One of his main conclusions was that in one pit management was trusted and in the other it was not. This is most people's experience. Anyone who has ever taken over responsibility for a number of factories will know what a difference there can be in their labour relations, and often the cause can be traced back quite clearly to good or bad management.

The trades union officer does not look for softness in bargaining. What he does look for is honesty, and to be treated on an equal footing and not with contempt or indifference. If management cannot concede a point it is better to say so rather than try to conceal it. The unions' advice to management would be, 'Don't be tricky, and don't be brutal'. In the words of St Peter, 'Honour all men'.

As far as the professional bodies are concerned, it has been traditional in Britain that, although they look after the interests of their members and in some cases negotiate salary levels with the government, they should never improve their bargaining power by a threat to strike. This has partly been because, until the nationalization of medicine, a profession was not confronted by a single employer, and the occasion did not arise. It was also partly because a profession embodies an ideal of disinterested public service, and it was hard to see how this sense of public duty could be reconciled with a threat to deprive the public of their professional skill. It is nevertheless true that unless professional earnings are tied in some way to the earnings of those who feel free to bargain, the professions, particularly those whose salaries are fixed by the government, will be at an increasing disadvantage.

Because of specialized skill, the professional is in an exceptionally strong position, and his instinct against using his whole bargaining strength is undoubtedly right. But if the community is so weak-willed that it concedes an improved share in its wealth only to those who threaten it, then the professional may need to reconsider his position. He owes a duty to the future to see that the right quality of man continues to be attracted into the profession in the right numbers, and if the differential for six years of hard training is not enough to do this, the public will suffer in the long run. It may still be undesirable to use his whole strength, but it may not be wrong for him to devise some means by which he can withdraw his services to the extent of creating embarrassment without doing lasting damage to those to whom he owes a duty of care. It is very much to be hoped, however, that the professions will never be brought to this pass, and the Christian will be anxious to devise alternative means of dealing with the situation which cause hurt to no-one and do no injury to the ethos of a professional service. To threaten to strike may be only the resort of professions which will not trouble to work out better methods.

CHAPTER SIX

THE AUTHORITY OF GOVERNMENT

UNTIL the last century, the government had little part to play in business. But since then industry has grown in size, rising incomes have raised economic expectations, and governments, particularly democratic governments, have had to pay increasing attention to economic affairs. Anyone in industry and commerce today will become involved sooner or later in government regulation, consultation and exhortation, not to mention taxation. What is to be our attitude as Christians to government activity? Should we welcome it, oppose it, or just wish it would go away?

There is a strong tradition in industry which deplores government interference of any kind, not only on practical, but also on moral grounds. Many Christians find the whole apparatus of politics and government distasteful, at best worldly, and at worst, in its use of the law and of force, a denial of the Sermon on the Mount. Added to this, there is a restless spirit in the world today. Its heroes are the resistance leaders and revolutionaries. From non-cooperation to fiddling tax, we are 'agin the government'. However strong these feelings may be, they are not in accordance with Christian teaching.

Government and the family are the only secular institutions which have been ordained by God. As Paul says in Romans 13, 'Let every soul be subject unto the higher powers. For there is no power but of God'. Our Lord has told us to 'Render therefore unto Caesar the things which are Caesar's'. But He also adds, render 'unto God the things that are God's'. Where there is a conflict between these two commands, the Christian must clearly obey God. But direct conflict seldom, if ever, comes in countries whose laws have been permeated by Christian principles, and even in other countries most people, for most of the time, are content to be subject to the authority of 'the powers that be'.

Those who feel that our ideal in political activity should be the commandment of our Lord in the Sermon on the Mount, 'resist not evil', misunderstand the Sermon; this is directed not to the nations of the world but to the Christian, and even then, not to the Christian in his capacity as a citizen, but in his personal relations. The world is, as we argued in the Introduction, under the law of God and its lawlessness must be controlled and its vice kept within bounds. God's means of doing this is the institution of government, and the Christian, in giving obedience to government, is giving obedience to God's chosen instrument. This is made quite clear in the passage from Romans 13 quoted above, and in 1 Peter 2, 'Submit yourselves to every ordinance of man for the Lord's sake: whether it be to the king, as supreme; or unto governors, as unto them that are sent by him for the punishment of evildoers, and for the praise of them that do well.' These passages do not accord with the view that the Christian should not resist evil in any form, and any interpretation of the Sermon on the Mount which does not take them into account must be suspect. It is clear that Paul regarded it as his right to claim the authority of Roman law to avoid wrongful imprisonment at Philippi and to enable him to appeal to the emperor. But Paul, who resisted evil intended against him by those outside the Church, made it clear to the Corinthian Christians that they should put up with harm from those within the Church, rather than submit their claims to non-Christian judges.

Paul, in Romans 12:19, tells us that Christians should not take vengeance, and then, in Romans 13:4, he says that the power is a 'minister of God . . . , a revenger to execute wrath upon him that doeth evil', and we are told to obey the power, and by implication, to help him in his task. The Christian may, therefore, in his capacity as a citizen have to do something quite out of keeping with the conduct of a Christian in his personal relationship. At least he is (verse 7) to pay taxes so that the police force will do it for him.

Other Christians can see some point in being subject to a democratically-elected government, but cannot see that it is right to be subject to a tyranny. This is a particularly important point for those who have relations with foreign governments which are certainly not all democratic. Are we, they ask, to say that the Huguenots who fought for their liberty in France, the Dutch Protestants who gained their liberty from the Spaniards under William the Silent were all in error, not to mention the Scots under John Knox, the Parliamentarians who rose against Charles I and the Whigs who forced James II's abdication? Had all those people been forced to the point where they would have had to disobey God if they obeyed the government? Were they not also contending, quite properly, for civil liberties? These are fair questions.

The Christian must, of course, disobey commands which conflict with specific Christian teaching. The three Jewish princes were right in refusing to bow down to the idol set up by Nebuchadnezzar. Daniel was right to continue to pray to his God, despite the laws of the Medes and Persians to the contrary. In our own day, it is inconceivable that a Christian could have been right to obey the state in killing six million Jews who had not offended against its laws. We are commanded to obey because the power was 'the minister of God to thee for good' and 'to execute wrath upon him that doeth evil'. If the power is a minister of evil it has, to that extent, lost its authority. But this necessary limitation does not detract from the authority of government in mundane affairs, and certainly not in the industrial affairs with which we are primarily concerned.

In these days when rebellion against authority is commonplace and seems, from the dislike of discipline and constraint, to gain general approval, we need to be particularly careful in justifying rebellion and revolution. The religious revolutions of the seventeenth century, however right they may have been, disturbed the general acceptance of the authority of government. They may even, to this extent, have paved the way for the much more thorough-going revolutions which had nothing to do with religious liberty and which have played some part in the general revolutionary mood of so much of the world in our own day.

When we look at the religious revolutions in detail, we become aware that the leaders realized that they had to justify themselves in relation to the Christian doctrines of civil obedience. In the case of the Huguenots, William the Silent, the Parliamentarians and the Protestant states in the Thirty Years War there was, as well as a very real fear for religious liberty, some legitimate question as to the identity of the 'powers that be'. In France, the Huguenots argued that the powers claimed by the king were an innovation (*Vindiciae contra tyrannus*, 1579). The Low Countries claimed that they were entitled to obey the 'Stadtholder' rather than the emperor. Even so, such was the respect for law and authority that William the Silent long maintained the fiction of loyalty to the emperor. John Hampden argued that the king was not entitled to impose a particular tax without consent of Parliament. The king alone was not the 'powers that be'. Even so, the Parliamentarians long maintained the fiction of loyalty to Charles. In Germany it was held that the power resided in the states and not in the emperor. These Protestant heroes cannot, therefore, without serious qualification be cited as examples of the right of minorities to disobey government.

In these days of nation states and written constitutions sovereignty is much more clearly defined, and cases where it would be right for a Christian to rebel or resort to force on grounds of disputed sovereignty would seem to be limited. There is certainly no case for taking direct action against a government on the sole ground that it is not democratic. The Roman Empire, under whose rule our Lord and Paul and Peter laid down the general rule of civil obedience, was far from democratic. Christians may prefer democracy and need not pretend otherwise, but in mundane matters they are bound by the laws of the land.

The Christian in industry, when inclined to disagree with his own or another government, must realize that however wrong-headed or arbitrary government action may seem, he is bound to obey it and support it. This is important, not only in relation to increasing involvement by the government in industry, but in relation to trade in newly-independent countries whose governments need every ounce of support if they are to do their job.

In an imperfect world there will be many cases where a Christian – as a Christian – is out of sympathy with the actions of a government or even with the whole system of government. Even if he is bound, as he is, by the laws of the land, he may well feel that it is his duty, within these limits, to oppose whatever he considers wrong. But whatever the wrong, there are certain rules he should follow. First, in his own country, he must act as a citizen. Just as we argued in an earlier chapter that he should not use the influence and authority of the Church so, on a lesser plane, he should not use any economic power he may have as an industrialist. The purpose of a company is to trade and not to rule. The same goes for trades unions, which should not use their power for political ends.

Second, his opposition to the policies of the government of a country in which he is not a citizen should be strictly limited to whatever concerns his business there, and should be conducted within the legal and social framework of opposition in that country. Third, where there is room for differing opinions, he should take advice from responsible men who are qualified to give it before he launches out. The many newly-independent countries are especially sensitive to alien economic dominance and see it as a very real threat to their independence. The Christian may be more tempted than most men to interfere, if only because he has high ideals and a sense of responsibility, but however right he may be he must respect and obey the government of the land in letter and in spirit, and he can only do harm to his Faith if he does not.

In an earlier chapter we dealt with the general relation of the government to industry and commerce, the case for and against both nationalization and the market economy. Most of our relationship with the government is on a much more humdrum level than this. The majority of

Christians might well agree with the earlier argument against an undue concentration of direct control in the hands of any authority, state or otherwise. But the line must be drawn somewhere. There are areas where an incorrupt and efficient state or local authority can render a better service than competing private interests. There are places where its powers are absolutely essential, not only to provide services which should be communal, but also to enforce standards of health and hygiene and of law and order. Everyone knows the exasperation which can be caused by petty officialdom and the absurdities of long out-dated bye-laws, and it is sometimes taken for granted that there was once an era of freedom when a man's life was his own, when he did very well indeed without the fussing bureaucrat. If anyone were forced to be precise, they might say that they thought that the rot set in during the First World War. Perhaps this attitude is now more common on the other side of the Atlantic than on this, but there is still a lot of feeling here that any government interference in industrial affairs is, almost of necessity, bad.

In any case, the idea of a golden age of complete *laissez-faire* is almost certainly a myth. According to G. Kitson-Clark (*The Making of Victorian England*), the British government started to try to bring industry under some sort of regulation well before the Industrial Revolution had gained full force. He regards 1833 as the turning-point when an act was passed 'which contained provision for the appointment of a board of inspectors with executive powers to put it into effect and to report on the way in which the Act worked'. The reports were the beginning of the specialized knowledge of government experts, and the discretionary power was the beginning of delegated powers given to ministers 'to be in fact exercised by civil servants'. 'Though the tremendous power which was being developed by the Industrial Revolution could and did work for the good of humanity, there could be no security that that was what it would do unless it was brought under conscious discipline, and that discipline could only be imposed by the assumption by the public of constantly increasing discretionary powers to be exercised under the direction of experts, who would draw upon growing experience which only work in that particular department of government could give'. The day of the specialized and powerful civil service department had begun.

The creation of an infra-structure of health and sanitation was necessary to avoid disaster, 'but without conscious direction, privately directed industrial development was most unlikely to do any of these things . . . . Power and knowledge to discipline and to direct and utilize these forces (of the Industrial Revolution) was needed if life was to be lived in tolerable conditions, let alone to improve in quality. That power could only be developed and directed to the right ends by the public authority'. So next time the planning authorities are being particularly maddening about some point, vital to us and apparently academic to them, we perhaps ought to reflect that they have been there, and rightly so, since the beginning of industrialization, and nothing is likely to be gained by wishing them away. We can only try to see that they fulfil their proper role better; and this may not mean any loosening of their control or slackening of their inquisitiveness.

If these points on the role of nineteenth-century government appear to have been somewhat laboured it is only because there is a not unnatural tendency among Christians to regard views held in a God-fearing church-going age as a norm, and any departure from them as being necessarily for the worse. It is just as well, therefore, to remind ourselves that one of the promoters of the 1833 Act and much of the subsequent legislation was that great Christian and Evangelical Lord Shaftesbury.

It is especially the rights of a government in waging war that have caused most controversy between Christians, and this is a very practical concern of most Christians in industry. With defence expenditure running at the rate of over £1,500m. a year and taking a very large proportion of the national product, there is hardly one industry which is not concerned with armaments in one way or another. Some industries are almost wholly devoted to it. This is not the place to tackle the pacifist issue. Many fine Christians have been pacifists and their point is clear-cut. 'Thou shalt not kill' is, for them, an absolute obligation without any complicated qualifications. One must respect them for this position and in Britain, as in other democratic countries, they are respected. But others feel that if the Sermon on the Mount does not preclude the maintenance of law and order nationally, it cannot preclude it internationally. In both cases law has to be backed by the sanction of force. There can, of course, be wars of aggression on an international scale, just as there can be tyranny on a national scale; but this does not affect the principle. The Christian's anxiety, as a citizen, will be to find a way out of international conflict other than war. A country governed by Christian ideals would not be jingoistic, would not throw its weight around light-heartedly and would not allow itself to be swept into conflict on a wave of fear or hate. But should it, in a world far from innocent, deprive itself of all power of resistance to its enemies? Should it not rather use its power to promote peace? The Pax Romana and Pax Britannica were not unworthy contributions to humanity.

The new dimension in war today is the weapon of mass-destruction. That nuclear weapons do introduce a new dimension to war can hardly be in doubt. Whereas civilians have been killed in previous wars, it was, in theory (even if mass-bombing had made the theory latterly a little remote from practice), possible to direct weapons almost exclusively at military targets. With the use of atomic weapons this is no longer possible. One must, again, respect the views of those who are not pacifists and are therefore prepared to make and use conventional military weapons, but who would sooner be defeated than make or use weapons of indiscriminate mass-destruction, whether atomic, gas or germ. It would be wrong for any individual in this novel and most difficult question to say that his sense of Christian values was the only right one, though it is a question on which, since it vitally affects all of us, it is particularly hard to be tolerant. This discussion has gone on endlessly over the last few years and there is little point in prolonging it here. There does seem to be a case both ways and it would be wrong automatically to condemn a Christian because he was engaged, directly or indirectly, in the manufacture of atomic weapons or the means of their delivery. His hope, as a Christian, would almost certainly be that in manufacturing them he was making more certain that they would never be used by either side. The fact is that many Christians engage in such work with a good conscience. We may disagree with their judgment, but we should not impute wrong motives.

Whether we like it or not, those of us in industry are a part of the whole national effort, including defence. There are strong grounds in Christian teaching for holding that a country is entitled to defend itself. Although there are many Christian pacifists, most Christians believe that the teaching in Romans 13 and 1 Peter 2 forces them to help the government in a number of tasks which are distasteful but are necessary to maintain order in the world. If we accept this we ought not to grudge our cooperation, but should participate actively and on principle. This does not exclude our exercising our rights as citizens to make constructive criticism of foreign and defence policies. We should see that the power of arms is used to promote peace and to minimize conflict.

There is an increasing tendency today for the government to bring pressure on industry without putting it under direct legal obligation. Sometimes these pressures and exhortations (for instance, to export) involve some measure of personal sacrifice or inconvenience with the aim of benefiting the community as a whole. In such cases, the Christian's duty is clearly to act in his neighbour's interest.

At other times, the government may decide to bring pressure to bear on industry to devote scarce resources to one purpose rather than another. Though, in general, Christian doctrine weighs the scale in favour of authority, nevertheless if the government's choice appears to be misguided or misinformed those in industry are not bound absolutely. The very fact that it is a matter for exhortation and not for legislation may reflect some uncertainty on the part of the government on the details of application in particular cases and a willingness, therefore, to leave the application in the end to individual judgment.

It is not always possible to act on exhortation if competitors refuse to do so, and there is no point in voluntary limitation of dividends if takeover bidders are free to buy the shares at a depressed price and put up the dividend as soon as they have gained control. But it is at the very least required by the Christian's respect for the 'powers that be' that he tries to discover the reason for the exhortation and behaves as sympathetically with its spirit as he can.

However strong the feeling against government interference in industry, it does not seem to stop the flow of requests to the government to do something to help particular industries. Nor is there anything wrong with this in principle. The industry ought to be the first to know when foreign rivals have gained an edge on it and when its employees' jobs are in danger. This may be because of the industry's own inefficiency, but it may just as well have to do with the international tariff structures or the creation by other governments of protected industries. Even in less dramatic circumstances, it is right and proper that if there is conflict between different groups of citizens there should be representation to government so that it can act as judge between them. What is necessary, however, is that those who put forward sectional interests should do so in accordance with the best standards of advocacy. All special interests should be declared. Information should not be misleading or put forward in a misleading way. But having declared our interests, we are entitled to put forward whatever arguments we consider should be taken into account, even though our interests would benefit should the decision go in our favour.

For instance, a group of shopkeepers are doing nothing wrong if they band together in an attempt to preserve amenities necessary to the continued use of their street as a shopping centre, even if this means the diversion elsewhere of heavy lorry traffic and an improvement in their property values. On a larger scale, an industrial district is entitled to represent to the government the consequence of the closing down of a major plant in its district, even if their remedy involves the diversion of government orders from plants in other districts.

Advocacy is not, however, the same thing as pressure, and the essence of a pressure group is, presumably, pressure. Is it right to bring pressure on an elected government? Is this not an avoidance of the agreed method of government? This very much depends on the method of pressure. If this is exercised through the open method of public debate or even through a statement that unless action is taken the matter will be made public, then this is not, in a democracy, avoidance of the democratic process, but a proper use of it. It is perfectly proper to point out to an individual member of parliament or to a government the possible electoral consequences of their actions. Pressure of vested interests is normally thought of, however, as something more sinister and powerful. What people rightly resent and regard as wrong is an attempt to go behind the issue in question and exercise some power over the government which has nothing to do with the real issue and which cannot be countered by the other side. Universal franchise limits the powers available to vested interests, but both trades unions and big business can exercise some pressure by refusal to cooperate in areas where government badly needs active help and support. This is as wrong as to threaten direct action to sabotage the action of government.

There are other powers which are nonetheless real for being harder to pin down. The power of patronage possessed by big business is perhaps the least of these, if only because its dangers are so well understood and the rules are fairly precise. The most dangerous, because the most subtle, is the power of social pressure, and one cannot do better than to put it in the words of a Memorial Oration by C. S. Lewis to students of King's College, London:

To nine out of ten of you the choice which could lead to scoundrelism will come, when it does come, in no very dramatic colours. Obviously bad men, obviously threatening or bribing, will almost certainly not appear. Over a drink or a cup of coffee, disguised as a triviality and sandwiched between two jokes, from the lips of a man, or woman, whom you have recently been getting to know rather better and whom you hope to know better still – just at the moment when you are most anxious not to appear crude or naive or a prig – the hint will come. It will be the hint of something which is not quite in accordance with the technical rules of fair play; something which the public, the ignorant romantic public, would never understand; something which even the outsiders in your own profession are apt to make a fuss about; but something which 'we always do'. And you will be drawn in, if you are drawn in, not by desire for gain or ease, but simply because, at that moment, when the cup was so near your lips, you cannot bear to be thrust back again into the cold outer world. It would be so terrible to see the other man's face – that genial, confidential, delightfully sophisticated face – turn suddenly cold and contemptuous, to know that you have been tried for the Inner Ring and rejected.

However wrong the recipient of social pressure may be if he acts for fear or favour, he may be deluded and not have the sense to know what is going on, but the man who exercises the pressure knows perfectly well what is going on and should know too that it is wrong.

Unfair social pressure can be used to obtain business and to exact influence in other walks of life, but the government is peculiarly susceptible to it and suffers maximum damage from it. The worlds of government and industry are becoming increasingly interwoven, and the problems we have looked at here can only give some indication of the kind of problems which arise for the Christian in industry in his relations with government, but they do serve to bring out the general principles on which these problems might be tackled. Human government, even if far from ideal, is ordained of God. However much we may dislike or disagree with its actions or its representatives, it is a divine institution and we must respect it.

CHAPTER SEVEN

'RENDER UNTO CAESAR'

ALTHOUGH the raising of taxes is a matter of legislation rather than of personal conduct, there are a number of reasons why it would be wrong to leave the subject out of account in a book like this. The state probably makes its greatest impact on most of us in its requirement that we pay to it a substantial proportion of our income, and the Christian's personal reaction to this requirement is important, both to himself and others. Avoidance and evasion are widespread. The Christian must know the principle on which he himself should act, both in a personal capacity and in his official capacity as a trustee for others. But, personal problems apart, the system of taxation as we know it was devised at a time of strong Christian influence. The amount to be raised in taxes and the methods of raising it are based as much on moral principles as on administrative convenience. When people talk of the iniquitous burden of taxation or the justice of taxing those who can afford it, they are talking in moral terms and basing their views on moral principles. Taxation today is an instrument for the application of principles of work and wealth and social justice, and if we do not want to find ourselves bound by law based on principles alien to our faith, it is as well that we should think out the place of Christian principles and uphold them as and when we have opportunity to do so. In any case, the world will judge us on our attitude to these moral problems. The faith for which we are told by the apostle Paul to give reason is not confined to the doctrine of salvation, but includes doctrines of conduct and morality. These are questions we cannot and should not evade.

For the Christian there is no doubt about the absolute right of the state to raise taxes, whether it is democratically elected or is an alien tyranny. We are told by our Lord to 'render therefore unto Caesar the things which are Caesar's' and He Himself set an example by paying His due tribute to the alien ruler. We are told (Romans 13) to render 'tribute to whom tribute is due'. The state is ordained by God and has certain rights over its citizens, of which this is one of the most important – important enough for specific instructions by our Lord Himself. In a democracy we do not even have the excuse put by the Jews, that it was wrong for the Lord's people to pay money to an alien tyrant.

Some of the citizens' needs are met from payments by the state from tax revenue and some directly from the individual's personal income. Where the line is drawn depends partly on custom and partly on moral principles. The cost of law and order and external defence has been met for so long by the state that it is hard to remember that powerful citizens once had private retainers who protected their interests and those of their dependants. Today many people feel that state expenditure has gone so far that it has sapped the moral fibre of the nation, but this extension was itself made on grounds of moral welfare. There is no doubt as to the Christian principle that the needs of the individual should be the first charge on his own family, and the individual Christian has no right to shuffle his responsibility off on to the state so long as he is capable of meeting it himself. Similarly, the Church has an obligation to look after those of its members who are in genuine need. But if a family cannot or will not fulfil its responsibility, then there is a strong case for saying that the citizens, through the state, have a residual responsibility.

The state, like the family, is a divinely ordained institution, put there for the restraint of evil and for the promotion of the common good of society. In doing this, it does not need to administer the details of the life of the citizen. If voluntary bodies undertake the task, the state can withdraw. Its responsibility is fulfilled when it sees that what needs to be done is done by itself or by someone else. For instance, it is not necessary for the state to provide compensation for all those injured in car accidents. It is considered sufficient to see that all car owners themselves pay for insurance cover and are heavily penalized if they do not. The state pension scheme is not compulsory, but the state requires that the employee is covered by a comparable scheme. To say that the state has a duty of care is not to say that it has a duty to tax and pay out in every detail of a citizen's life. But in some things, such as the maintenance of law and order, it is patently better, at least in society as it is today, for the state itself to administer.

In practice, boundaries of state expenditure have been set by the anxiety on the one hand that every citizen should have the right to vital goods and services (including education, housing and medical care without the indignity of a means test), and, on the other hand, that too much 'laid on' regardless of individual effort will be bad for moral fibre. There is something in both points. Over-anxiety for moral fibre led to the Victorian workhouse, and since that time the trend has been almost entirely the other way. But the welfare service is now so universal that it has, in turn, attracted the weight of criticism. There is a feeling that the limit of public service has been reached, and that for the universal welfare state should be substituted a welfare 'safety net' to catch those in real want leaving those who do not require it to look after themselves. Various methods have been suggested of having a means test without subjecting the individual to an inquisition by strangers into his private affairs. The income tax coding gives a rough general guide to a man's means, though the numbers who do not pay tax might make this too wide a net. The Australian medical service is run on the basis that the patient has his medical fees refunded partly by the state and partly by compulsory medical benefit societies.

In medicine, the old panel system provided a safety net, but many who were poor but independent suffered rather than go on the panel and accept what they considered to be charity. The good panel doctor was second to none, and his patients did not suffer, but the system depended perhaps more heavily than the National Health Scheme on the integrity of the individual doctor. Those who require the safety net are not all wage earners, capable of responding to a dose of moral fibre. A large proportion would be wives, children and the very old. Any move away from free education could fall harshly on the able children of poor parents. Any move away from children's allowances would fall harshly on wives and children of those husbands and fathers who would not make good the amount. The safety net theory might control wasteful expenditure, but at some cost to the happiness of those who cannot look after themselves.

It seems logical to suppose that there must be some upper limit to the proportion of national income which can be taken in taxation, some point at which there is a sharply diminishing return for extra imposts. But one generation's predicted limit can seem absurdly low to the generation after. Government expenditure was 10 per cent of the Gross National Product immediately before the First World War. Between the wars it rose to 20 per cent, and since the war it has varied between 36 per cent and 40 per cent. In 1910, when the House of Lords felt so strongly about increased taxation that it put its power and position at risk in the fight, income tax was 1s. 2d. in the £ and the proposed supertax was to be 6d. in the £ on incomes over £5,000.

Perhaps a better guide than moral indignation is the growth of avoidance and evasion. Beyond a certain point taxable income disappears either through legal avoidance or illegal evasion. Although taxes are now lower than they were immediately after the war, there is some evidence that a high level of taxes sustained for so long has begun this process. No-one can be complacent about this, particularly since avoidance and evasion bring the rule of law itself into contempt. If the rule of law, which is the basis of an ordered society, is to be maintained, then legislation must have general support. It is this requirement which, in the world as it is, places a practical limit on the extent to which men's affairs can be subjected to legislation. If we find that taxation beyond a certain level brings avoidance and evasion, then that is a guide to the practical upper limit of taxation.

The quickest solution to the need to finance a growing level of public expenditure would be a proportionate or more rapid rise in national taxable income. This would pay for the expenditure without extra taxes. But in the long run it may be necessary to find some way in which to reinvigorate the check on public expenditure which used to be exercised to some effect by parliament.

Adam Smith laid down four famous canons of taxation: 1. Taxation should be equal (on equal incomes) or proportional to income. 2. Tax levies should not be uncertain or arbitrary. 3. Taxes should not be exacted in an inconvenient manner. 4. Taxes should be economical to collect. It is interesting to note that the first two, which are the most important, have a moral basis. In fact, almost any general principle of taxation must be established on grounds such as fairness, justice and duty. The Christian would probably accept the principle that taxation should be equal, in the sense that all taxpayers in similar circumstances should bear an equal tax burden. If we are to love our neighbour as ourselves we should not wish him to bear a burden which, in similar circumstances, we would not be prepared to bear ourselves. This principle means that every distinction in the tax structure should have some reasonable justification and be fair as between taxpayers. It also means that loopholes creating artificial distinctions should be closed by legislation as they become evident. Tax concepts such as 'income' and 'earned income' should be defined accurately, realistically and truthfully.

Whereas it was necessary for Adam Smith, in his day, to argue that taxes should be proportional to income (i.e. the rate of tax should be equal), the present principle is that taxes should be progressive (i.e. at an increasing rate for increasing incomes). There are arguments against progressive taxation, but they are not always as strong as they seem. Progressive taxation may have been a major factor in increasing the level of gross salaries, since the steep gross differentials in the higher ranges would not seem functionally necessary except for the provision of noticeable net differentials. Even where they are functionally necessary they often reflect the shortage of a particular skill rather than extra training or responsibility, and progressive taxes take back for the community something of the extra amount made by the man who has made a temporary 'corner' in that skill. However, it is one thing to accept progression as a general principle and another to agree with a very high rate of progression. Steep progression on income places an effective ceiling on income and is equivalent to saying that no-one, however skilled or responsible, however hazardous his job, or however temporary the income, deserves to earn more than so much in a year. This is not a proposition which most people would defend as fair, and it is certainly one which no union negotiator, arguing on differentials, would accept for a moment.

If there is to be progressive taxation, it would seem fairer to put a levy on expenditure rather than on income. Then, instead of saying that no-one *deserved* more than so much a year, the law would be saying that no-one *needed* more than so much a year, which would surely seem to be more susceptible to objective judgment. And if it is not possible to judge objectively about a man's needs, it is certainly not possible to judge what he deserves. Not only would it seem to be a fairer tax, but the moral case also seems stronger. It is surely better to tax a man on what he takes out of the community than on what he puts into it. The effect of the present system is to treat accumulated wealth lightly, but to tax new savings heavily. This freezes society into its present stratification and increases the dependence of wage and salary earners on those who have inherited accumulated wealth. It would seem more just to tax new savings relatively lightly and to put the weight on expenditure. Luxurious expenditure takes a disproportionate and unnecessary share of goods and services; it is both depraving and a social evil.

There is at present a steeply progressive rate of death duty and a steeply progressive rate of taxation on incomes, slightly higher on unearned incomes than on earned incomes. In theory, this taxes the rich at a higher rate than the poor. In practice, its effects in wide areas are almost exactly the opposite. Death duties can be avoided completely by a transfer of property five years before death and income taxes hardly matter when there is no tax on the annual capital gains (which, in well-managed companies, should be almost guaranteed by the current high rates of ploughed-back profits). If properly run, the average estate, even those which have not used income-spreading devices like discretionary trusts, must have given its beneficiaries greater absolute increases in wealth, to spend or to save, than at any time previously. It is worthy of note, too, that the larger the estate, the better it is able to afford advisers who will maximize its wealth and minimize its taxes. The person with a high earned income but no inherited capital can never under present tax legislation, except by a freak, attain the ranks of the wealthy which are now almost closed to newcomers. A tax system which maintains such exclusivity of wealth can hardly be described as just, nor can it in the long run command respect.

An expenditure tax in place of surtax and at a lower rate of progression than the present surtax would effectively reform the present inequities. Roughly speaking, annual expenditure would be arrived at by deducting the year's increase in assets from income or adding the decrease to income. If gifts were excluded from expenditure, it would also be necessary to have a gifts tax to prevent the present avoidance of death duties, but there would seem to be no reason, if the rate of progression were lower, to exclude gifts from expenditure. The feasibility of this kind of expenditure tax has been expounded by Nicholas Kaldor, in his book *An Expenditure Tax*. Its main requirement is an annual declaration of capital as well as of income, but this has to be done for capital gains taxes (to which this is an alternative), and is at present done in the Scandinavian countries for their capital taxes. It might also require some averaging of exceptional expenditure, but this should be no more complex than the present fairly simple rules for averaging exceptional income for authors. Combined with an effective gifts tax in place of death duties, this would allow all saving during a man's lifetime to be exempt from surtax, but would effectively break up large estates now passing intact more than five years before death. It would therefore reverse the present incidence of taxation in favour of earned income rather than inherited capital.

As with so many attempts at moral equity, it does add some complication, but if moral equity is what people want – and it is what we should want – then the additional complications are a small price to pay.

Some measure of redistribution of capital would seem to be in accordance with the Christian view of wealth which we discussed in an earlier chapter. While great wealth may be used to good purpose, it may also be used to exploit or to exercise power over others, and may be used for ostentatious display which can only aggravate social conflict. Redistribution does not, it must be granted, add much to the wealth of the many, for the very reason that they are many and the great fortunes are spread over the few. But it may well be that what is added is of more significance to the poor man, woman or child who gains it than the rich man who gives it up. Any marginal increase in income matters a lot to anyone living at or about subsistence level. It also matters a lot to a backward country trying to make the first economic advances, where it may well raise its people above subsistence level.

There are limits to redistribution. If we follow the logic of our earlier arguments, it should not go so far as to subject the proceeds of taxes to the law of diminishing returns. It should be aimed against the accumulation over generations of powerful fortunes rather than hamper the creation of wealth by taking away from a man each year most of what his own efforts have earned him in that year. Labour and reward are linked in Christian teaching and tax structures should not be so extreme as virtually to destroy this association.

Taxation has not only been used for social redistribution, it has also traditionally been used to damp down certain types of expenditure where excess has been considered socially undesirable. This has been done by high flat-rate sales taxes, mainly on drink and tobacco, and latterly on betting. There is little doubt that cheap gin was a social disaster. 'Drunk for a penny, dead drunk for twopence, clean straw free' was a slogan which reflected real conditions. Hogarth drew from life and not from imagination. Evidence of the effects of cigarette smoking puts it into a similar category. At the other end of the scale, there has always been a strong reluctance to impose any taxes on food, and this is one of the strongest arguments against a flat-rate sales tax. Both these positions seem basically right. On the other hand, as Sir Gerald Nabarro has demonstrated, in his series of detailed questions in the House of Commons, the system of varied rates of purchase tax, classing some goods as luxuries and others as essentials, can be made to look very silly and smacks rather too much of bureaucratic paternalism for most people's liking. One of the advantages of a progressive expenditure tax in place of surtax is that it would have the desired social effect without the paternalism and absurdity of differential purchase tax.

Most countries place more emphasis on flat-rate taxes on expenditure than on general taxes on income. The argument for them is that they are easier to assess and more difficult to evade. There is a further argument, that they can be used more precisely than income taxes to control inflationary and deflationary cycles in the economy. The main moral objection to them is that they are regressive (*i.e.* the less income you have, the higher the proportion you pay in tax), and in addition if they are to include necessities like food then this is a definite objection. It is in principle, as we have argued, more just to tax expenditure than income; to tax a man on what he takes out rather than what he puts in. But the case for this tax is not so strong as for the progressive expenditure tax on individuals. As lower incomes rise and its regressive effects matter less, the case will become stronger, but at the moment the pros and cons are nicely balanced.

As far as tax evasion is concerned, for the Christian there is no problem. It is illegal and he must not do it. The problems arise from what is called 'avoidance', which is the arrangement of one's affairs in such a way as to minimize liability to tax. This is his legal right. It is expressed in a number of legal judgments. Lord Clyde, a Scottish judge, has said,

> No man in this country is under the smallest obligation, legal or other, so to arrange his legal relations to his business or to his property as to enable the Inland Revenue to put the largest possible shovel into his stores. The Inland Revenue is not slow – and quite rightly – to take every advantage which is open to it under the taxing statutes for the purpose of depleting the taxpayer's pocket. And the taxpayer is, in like manner, entitled to be astute to prevent, so far as he honestly can, the depletion of his means by the Inland Revenue.

In a leading House of Lords decision, Lord Sumner said,

> My Lords, the highest authorities have always recognized that the subject is entitled to arrange his affairs as not to attract taxes imposed by the Crown so far as he can do so within the law, and that he may legitimately claim the advantage of any express terms or of any omission that he can find in his favour in the taxing acts. In doing so, he neither comes under liability nor incurs blame.

This is the law in Britain. It is expressly recognized that there is no measure of fairness – what the law calls equity – in taxation. You are either in the letter of the statute and liable or outside and not liable. You cannot be excluded by pleading equity (the technical term for natural justice) and you cannot, therefore, be included by a Revenue plea of equity. The principle of equity applies to other branches of the law, but not to taxation.

This is not, however, quite the end of the matter. While it would be wrong to ask the Christian to set himself up as a judge on the fairness or unfairness of a point of law, he cannot proceed without the slightest recognition of the difference between various classes of avoidance or of the general effects of avoidance. That there are differences is recognized in a judgment by Lord Simon, when Lord Chancellor,

My Lords, of recent years much ingenuity has been expended in certain quarters to devise methods of disposition of income by which those who were prepared to adopt them might enjoy the benefits of residence in this country while receiving the equivalent of such income without sharing in the appropriate burden of British taxation. Judicial dicta may be cited which point out that however elaborate and artificial such methods may be, those who adopt them are 'entitled' to do so. There is, of course, no doubt that they are within their legal rights, but that is no reason why their efforts, or those of the professional gentlemen who assist them in the matter, should be regarded as commendable exercise of ingenuity or as a discharge of the duties of good citizenship. On the contrary, one result of such methods, if they succeed is, of course, to increase pro tanto the load of tax on the shoulders of the great body of good citizens, who do not desire, or do not know how, to adopt these manoeuvres.

There is a difference, for instance, between entering into life assurance policies in order to spread income into retirement, when it will be taxed at a lower rate, and systematic operation of the complex procedure known as 'bond-washing'. The one is taking advantage of a provision clearly intended for the purpose, the other is equally clearly driving a horse and cart through an accidental loophole. Few reasonable men would interpret the latter as being in the spirit of the law. All the transactions are highly artificial, and the provisions are being used for a purpose for which they were never intended.

The Christian has another principle which he can bring to bear in doubtful cases. This is that he should earn his living in a way befitting to a Christian. His livelihood should have some constructive purpose and spending his whole life in finding loopholes in the tax laws hardly fits this bill. There is a clear distinction between the work of the normal accountant who advises his clients on their tax and the man whose reputation depends on his skill in working out methods of sailing as close to the wind as possible.

Perhaps the most difficult cases are those where a tax which was clearly intended to be levied at certain rates on certain classes of people has become, through time, little more than a voluntary tax. Death duties are now decidedly in this class, and in certain circumstances surtax has almost reached it. Most people used to leave the bulk of their estate in their wills, and duties were assessed on the value of the estate at death. Now, stimulated no doubt by death duties, the bulk of a large estate is in almost all cases handed over in the lifetime of the owner. It makes very little difference to him, but a great deal of difference to the heirs, and so it has become the custom. Is the Christian to be the exception and stick to the old way when no-one else does? Without being dogmatic, it does seem that when there has been a decisive and widespread change in the arrangement of the financial affairs of individuals, when all responsible advisers, solicitors and accountants advise in the same way and when this is allowed by the government without any amendment or alteration in the law, then the intention of government can be presumed to have changed.

It would of course be very much better if the government changed the law. It may be politically convenient to have high nominal rates of taxation leaving the doors wide open to gifts during life, with tax-free capital gains and discretionary trusts to mitigate the practical effects of high rates. But it is not an entirely fair policy. Just as much tax would be levied if the rates were lower and the legislation effective. And it is better that legislation should be effective both for the citizen and for the law itself.

CHAPTER EIGHT

FAIR TRADING

T HERE is a strong trend today towards more competitive industry, and Britain's situation in the world is such that this is unlikely to be reversed. At the same time, there is a good deal of ignorance about what competition really means. Most people think of it as price competition, but there is competition, too, in advertising, design and in sheer persuasion. Even price competition is not straightforward. In the United States, where competition has long been held to be to the general benefit of society, a mass of legislation has been necessary to try to impose this simple concept in the vast variety of different situations which arise. Despite this formidable effort, few industrialists there seem to feel that the situation is entirely fair even now in meeting the complexities of price competition. But competition is held to be a major check on the power of capitalism, and anyone attempting to moralize must find out what it is and what it does.

The simple theory of price competition is that the man who can make a product cheaper than the next man is entitled to sell it cheaper and thereby to gain a larger share of the business. This helps to keep down the cost of goods, and is to the public benefit in stimulating the growth of the more efficient firms. The difficulty is that in practice the situation is almost always more complicated than this. Today costs are increasingly incurred not in payment of wages for daily output, but in the original installation of plant and machinery. This is the difference between variable cost and sunk cost. The higher the sunk cost, the greater the gulf between the average cost of production over a period of time and the cost of producing a marginal extra unit. In some very highly capitalized industries the average cost can be 80 per cent of selling price, giving an average profit of 20 per cent, and the marginal cost of an extra unit as low as 10 per cent, giving a marginal profit of 90 per cent. Here low costs depend as much on volume as on efficiency, and volume may well depend, in turn, almost solely on price. In these circumstances, the temptation is to keep a high price to the majority of customers and to gain extra business by price-cutting (in a limited section of the market). In the United States, this is regarded as unfair practice, and the general rule is that the seller should charge customers the same for the same product. But even this simple rule is hard to enforce, because the law allows a company to reduce the price to match a competitor's price rather than break its price structure or lose the business. This permits sellers to have one price for one customer and another price for another customer. It then becomes very difficult to tell who is making competition and who is matching it.

The fact of life is that it is very hard to control a flexible and fluid pricing situation with an inflexible instrument like legislation. This is not to deny that some sort of protection is necessary. Companies can not only be unfair as between their customers, but a large and powerful company can use differential pricing to discriminate against a particular competitor, cutting prices on the products made by the competitor either to bring it to heel or even to run it out of business. To control this situation requires, not the dead hand of statute law and legal precedent, but some body well informed on the economics of the industry and capable of holding the ring. This could be done by the industry sub-councils of NEDC suggested earlier. An impartial arbiter could also deal with genuine cases where lower costs gave an advantage to some companies and put the future of their competitors at risk. Very often an industry holds up prices in order to protect the weaker companies. No individual company has a particular responsibility to put up plans which would enable the industry to work its way out of such a situation, and even if one company did put up plans it might not be powerful enough to gain acceptance of its solution. The more one goes into the matter, the more the assumption that unsupervised competition will bring about the best possible result appears as a doctrinaire view based on long out-dated premises. It may have been appropriate to deal with an industry with many producers with low capitalization, but not with a few large companies with high capitalization.

While there is no referee to competition, the Christian who is in a position to decide trading policies will have to work out his own solutions as best he may. His guiding rule is the old one that he should treat others with the respect he would like to receive from them. On the other hand, while unfettered competition is the rule, he cannot concede a competitive advantage. If competition is tough he will have to be tough too. But if he has any influence in his industry, it should be exercised in a constructive way, to achieve what he thinks a fair solution, not only for the industry, but also for its customers. For example, he should not be content with a price policy which gives him a reasonable reward if the policy still allows customers to suffer from discriminatory pricing.

Where there is price competition, the profits which can be obtained will be governed by the competitive price level. But there are still times at which it will be necessary to set some objective standard for prices and profits. This is particularly the case in bringing out a new product. There is, of course, the cheerful unworried businessman whose philosophy is 'charge what the market will stand'. But aside from the social repercussions, this is not usually good business unless the company is going to wind up in the near future. High profits are likely in fairly quick time to attract competition, and in highly capitalized industries this can result in formidable over-capacity for a prolonged period.

Assuming that the costs of a product can be properly allocated, the factors in fixing the price are the price of money (the interest on capital), the rate of capital turnover (the relation between capital employed and turnover) and the risk factor (the risk over time of obsolescence of plant and product). These factors require a profit margin on unit price higher than most people outside industry will credit. To the outsider, industry may appear solidly established, even formidable in its dominance of the market. The man who has to stay in business in a competitive world, and who realizes the dependence of his work force on his decisions, sees the world as a much more hazardous place.

Perhaps the most controversial factor in the level of company profits is not so much the risk factor – which no-one with industrial experience will dispute – but the extent to which the company should use the profit revenue from its current products to finance its movement into other activities, instead of paying out to shareholders, customers and work force. Certainly there is a tendency on the part of companies to hang on to more money than is strictly necessary, and it is easy to see in the extreme cases that this is wrong. But the pattern of business does change over time, and the increasing rate of technical innovation requires a sufficient investment in research at least to keep abreast of change. It also requires sufficient cash in hand to get through a competitive rough patch when it may not be possible to find money on the market. Nor can a new product go on the market without teething troubles. The more highly capitalized the industry, the less likely the new product will be to recover its costs quickly. For a time new products have to be subsidized through profits on products whose costs have been reduced through long experience in manufacture. Profitability cannot really be assessed except over a period of years, and there have to be fat years to make up for the lean before price and margin are reduced as more competitors move into the field. In some industries where only a proportion of projects will get off the ground, those which do go well have to pay for those which do not.

Pricing is only one part of industrial competition. In inter-company selling, decisions are increasingly made on design, specification and general confidence in performance. The decision of individuals in the buying company can be of vital importance, and the knowledge that two or three individuals can be decisive in the placing of a multi-million pound order would seem to place strenuous demands on integrity as well as salesmanship.

A Christian's concern for the truth must be paramount, and it might seem at first sight that there would be a conflict between his obligation to be truthful and his desire to persuade the buyer. But this is not usually the problem it seems. Almost all industrial purchases are intended for a purpose. The purpose commonly requires a specification, and the specification is a matter of objective measurement. The seller knows perfectly well that if his machine is not up to specification it will be returned. There are, of course, claims which can be made on the margin, but a sophisticated industrial buyer is likely to know as much about his subject as the seller and, if he is any good at all, is unlikely to sign multi-million contracts – or indeed contracts for any amount – through misunderstanding as to what he is buying.

Apart from any moral standards, enlightened self-interest is likely to keep the seller to the truth. He will want to make and preserve his company's reputation. He will want the customer to come again, and the customer is unlikely to do this if he has been sold any species of pup. This is the kind of area in business where 'honesty is the best policy'. It is not, therefore, an area where the Christian should find himself in a serious moral dilemma. There are matters which do not go to the root of the contract where a Christian should earn a reputation as a man of his word. In the best-ordered businesses, there will be late deliveries. There will be strikes and unscheduled breakdowns against which there can be no guarantee. But the Christian should be as fair and accurate as he can in giving delivery dates. He should not consistently obtain business on delivery dates which are unlikely to be kept, and if there is some known hazard about delivery, he should say so.

The Christian who looks after his company's interests will be a tough negotiator. But there is a difference in people's minds between hard bargaining, which is considered fair, and hard bargains, which are not. The Christian should not earn the reputation of screwing the last ounce out of every situation. This much, at least, should be deduced from the parable of the unforgiving steward, who having been forgiven a major debt by his lord, was merciless in exacting a much smaller debt which someone else owed to him. It can be deduced, too, from the teaching on usury, the essence of which is that we should not take advantage of the temporary weakness of our neighbour. For instance, if a contract is entered into in good faith and circumstances arise which were not envisaged by either party, it is fairer to renegotiate than to press your legal rights to the detriment of the other party. The best City practice is that one should 'not be too greedy' and should always try to leave something in it for the other man. The man who wants to preserve a reputation in the City takes care never to leave a bad taste behind, and bears in mind that there is always another day and another deal. The Christian standard should certainly be no less than this.

Another aspect of this question is the amounts which should be spent in entertaining customers. The Christian should hardly need to discuss the worst abuses of expense accounts. Putting in for more than he has spent, with or without the connivance of his firm, is a fraud, if not on the firm, then certainly on the Inland Revenue. There is no problem. We are told to be honest and that is an end of the matter. Nor is there any problem in the entertainment of friends under guise of customers. This, too, is wrong.

The problem for the Christian is in the amount and kind of entertainment he should lay on for genuine customers. Having a meal with a customer is in itself a right and proper thing to do. We have to get to know the people with whom we are doing business, and an invitation to eat together is both a gesture of friendliness and an opportunity for better acquaintance. The abuse begins when the level of entertainment goes beyond what we would do for personal friends. Where entertainment is at a higher level than a man would expect, it begins to move away from the line which preserves the strict impartiality of the officer of the purchasing company. Taking a junior purchasing officer out to dinner in the smartest of night spots either affects his judgment, in which case it is wrong, or it does not affect it, in which case it is a waste of the company's money.

It may be difficult to decide the exact level of entertainment appropriate to a particular customer, but it should not be impossible. The Foreign Office has arrived over the years at a workable arrangement for different levels of entertainment. A fair guide is the standard of living of the giver and receiver of the hospitality. What would be a pleasant memory to a wealthy director could well be a bribe to an assistant purchasing officer. Conversely, the hospitality expected from the chairman of a company is bound to be greater than that offered by an individual salesman. What would seem wrong is the giving of entertainment at expensive establishments by individuals who would never dream of incurring that sort of bill on their own account for their friends or family. This is what the man in the street means when he complains of businessmen who are 'living it up on expense account'.

It is just a short step from this to outright bribery. The Bible clearly and specifically condemns the giving of gifts to judges, and although bribing a judge of law is more serious than bribing a man who has to judge between different tenders, the principle would seem to be the same. Fortunately, it is still possible to stay in business in our own country without bribery, although the Christian should be aware of the dangers and use his influence to maintain high standards of integrity. All of us tend to underestimate our own influence but the Christian especially should have some faith that if he acts as he should, his actions will not be ineffective. The real problem, however, comes in exporting to countries where little or no business can be transacted without gifts. Should the Christian avoid all business in these countries? There are degrees of gifts. There are those clearly intended to influence business. On the other hand, there are those which are accepted by certain as a supplementary salary in countries where civil servants are not given a living wage. These take the form of a local tax or toll. They are paid to the clerk for prompt clearance of documents; to the secretary for an appointment to see the Minister; to the harbourmaster for seeing goods through customs in reasonable time. These are all gifts on a small scale, do not pervert judgment, are known to the local government and the amounts payable are said to be obtainable, in many cases, from the local consular officers. It would seem to be slightly dogmatic to condemn all those who made this sort of payment, but for the sake of the integrity of local expatriate staff it is desirable that these payments should be covered in the agent's commission.

Bribery, in the accepted sense, is unfortunately widespread in many parts of the world. Those who will not engage in this business lose less than might appear. When a smooth gentleman turns up in London to say that President B wants to build a £12m. palace and that 10 per cent will obtain the order, it is high odds that nothing of the kind will happen. The first hazard is that the emissary will be a fraud, the second that the President has developed megalomania and will shortly be deposed. Even if both propositions are strictly factual, the chances are that the President and intermediary will want to borrow the entire cost and pay back at 3 per cent over 25 years. Let us suppose, for a moment, that by some extraordinary chance there is enough money in the national treasury, it is still more likely than not that there will be endless indecisive haggling the other end as to who gets what cut from the 10 per cent, and this can go on for ever without anyone being able to find out what is really happening. At the last moment, the whole scheme can be ditched by a bid from elsewhere for 12 per cent. Meantime, all sorts of good men, design staff and salesmen have wasted their time, and sound business elsewhere has been lost. The way of the transgressor is hard.

There appears to be little corruption in business dealings with communist countries, and the local communist parties in countries where there is corruption are strong both in their condemnation of such practices and of the behaviour of those from so-called Christian countries who help to maintain corrupt governments in power by such means. All bribes have to be recovered in the price charged to the customer, and the cost falls ultimately on the people of the country concerned. In some countries the business of bribing becomes so complicated, and there is so much dispute about the sharing of the proceeds, that major projects urgently required for welfare and material progress can get held up for years.

The first kind of payment, which is little more than an enlarged gratuity, seems unfortunately to be inevitable. But at least there is no element of perverting judgment. The Christian will want to keep this to the minimum, and should always pay strictly to the scale and never pervert judgment to obtain competitive advantage. Payment to pervert judgment is wrong whatever its scale and a Christian will want nothing to do with it. Unless things become much worse, this should not stop him from getting business, and indeed it may help him. But even if it did damage him, he should still hold back. Setbacks because of this will usually be only temporary; a good reputation may have to be built at the cost of such setbacks. Once built it will result in increased confidence from others and increased business. 'Them that honour me I will honour.'

But, apart from bribery, it is part of a salesman's job to use his powers of persuasion. There is nothing to be ashamed of in trying to convince a potential customer of the genuine merits of your product. But the salesman who has Christian standards sets himself limits. It is the Christian's absolute obligation not to tell lies. This includes both what he says and what he infers. He cannot tell everything about his goods, but what he omits must not make what he tells misleading. Secondly, the Christian must remember that his customer is a man created by God as a rational being and must be respected as such. We should appeal, therefore, to his reason and not to his subconscious. Thirdly, we must, particularly in personal encounter, respect the dignity and integrity of a man's personality. It is wrong for a strong personality to ride roughshod over a weaker one.

The manufacturer is faced with the facts of mass production and the consequent need of a mass market. As living standards rise and necessities take a lower proportion of income, an increasing proportion of manufacturing output goes in production of goods which people can buy or stop buying as they fancy. Consumer spending becomes more flexible. But in parallel, high living standards are brought about by higher capitalization, and this makes production less flexible. There are, therefore, the strongest possible pressures on businessmen to secure both standardization and continuity by standardizing demand and securing their customers' allegiance. Added to these pressures is our social desire to give people a choice and therefore to maintain competition between different manufacturers of the same product. These are the key factors in the rise of advertising.

Before judging too hastily on the 'waste' expenditure of advertising, it is as well to look behind the very high absolute figures. If there were no advertising this amount of money would not be saved. Newspapers, magazines and everything else subsidized by advertising would probably cost twice as much. Nevertheless, even allowing for this and for some brightness, zest and significance which good advertising can give to some of the chores of life, the cost in time and talent is undoubtedly high. Industry spends twice as much on advertising as on research. Both on social and economic grounds it is probably right to try to keep advertising within bounds. It is not always easy to see how this can be done. If a product is the subject of competitive advertising and one firm cuts its advertising expenditure, it will almost certainly lose market share. The best method for the Christian who thinks that advertising expenditure in his own industry is excessive and wasteful is to try to work with his competitors for a mutual reduction in the level.

Although there are obvious dangers in advertising, there is no need, in measuring them, to accept the advertising industry's own assessment of its effectiveness at face value. It is true that anyone who takes the trouble to think about the matter will, because he is accustomed to think, be less likely to be affected much by advertising, but even discounting this, there is evidence that the effectiveness of advertising on the human will is overstated. It is true that in competitive advertising brand switching is responsive to advertising volume, but what worries most people, particularly Christians, is not so much the plugging of brand names, but the pressure of appeals to the worst traits in human nature, like avarice and arrogance. If they were uniformly successful we would be entitled to be worried. But the fact is that they are not. People are patently a good deal less subject to pressure than advertisers will allow.

In America in the late fifties there was enormous expenditure by all the major motor manufacturers on advertising cars, which were larger, longer, more prestigeous and more powerful. To own last year's style was said to lead to social disaster. In fact, those cars which increased their share of the market most rapidly were the small imported cars with small engines and few trimmings, and the most popular was the Volkswagen, which had not changed its basic style since the nineteen-thirties. Social prestige went to the owner of the imported sports car which had no prestige build-up. The subject of one of the largest market research and promotional expenditures in motorcar history, the Edsel, was a complete flop. In Britain, BMC produced a small estate-car and gave it the very utilitarian title of the Morris Traveller, with the market for commercial travellers clearly in mind. It was very successful, not least as a second car for upper-income families who were not in the least put off by its name. If we are discussing the morality of advertising pressure, we may be discussing what people are trying to do. It does not follow that they are succeeding.

The other point worth making before we start to moralize is that most advertising is concerned with a straightforward description of the goods advertised. Almost all technical advertising is in this category. So is a great deal of advertising of consumer goods. Most clothing advertisements, for instance, have little more than a drawing or photograph, a price and a very short description. There are few moral problems here, provided the descriptions are not misleading; and, unless one thinks that people are really misled by the slight poetic licence, most descriptions would seem to be reasonable.

The moral problem begins to arise as one moves into the area where the real differences between competing products are insignificant. This includes the products of process industries which cannot be described except in technical terms unintelligible to the layman. Petrol and detergents are examples. Here there seems to be two different paths which companies can take. One is simply to concentrate on some positive identification of the product – a hall-mark which associates the advertisement with the product at the point of sale, but need hardly bother with a description. One of the best is the pre-war 'That's Shell that was' which survived in folklore long after it was dropped by the company (which now uses the more mundane 'You can be sure of Shell').

The other line, which seems less desirable, but hardly more effective, is to try to associate the product with some mood or attitude of the buyer. The advertiser tries to make the reader identify himself with the man or woman in the advertisement who is using the product, and the type of person projected is, not unnaturally, very much a man or woman of the world. As one critic puts it, 'Advertisement man is an urban good-looker with one unmistakable virtue, ambition. He is clearly on the way up, a coming top person, outstripping his fellows all the way along in clothes, girls, cars and cigarettes. He is a conformist, permanently inoculated against awkward critical hesitations or doubts'. On the other hand, many people's instinctive reaction against all the smug men in the advertisements is hostility rather than awe. Whether they really have a more sinister effect on any but the weakest minds is open to argument.

The Christian who has any say in advertising policy will almost certainly want to avoid advertisements which are undisguised appeals to covetousness or based on erotic appeal. But such is the range of human ingenuity that this ought not to cramp his style. He will also want to exercise the greatest care in the field of patent medicine. This is subject to legal restrictions, but there is probably a grey area within the letter of the law where claims, unless qualified, could be misleading.

Vance Packard in *The Hidden Persuaders* has illuminated the dangers of a lack of respect for human personality in advertising. Some of the reported advice given by the psychologists and motivational research men appears to be nothing but sound common sense. For instance, there is little in their reputed advice on the unfortunate 'image' of the Californian prune that is likely to worry the Christian. But their attitude to people is disturbing. The industrialist realizes that his ability to stay in business is partly dependent on the irrational whims of the buyer, and a desire to guard against these irrationalities has led some companies to get advice from psychologists. But it is one thing to defend yourself against irrationalities. It is quite a different affair to exploit them. There is no doubt that people do have an 'image' of a company or a product and this may be quite irrational. For instance, one understands that the traditional delicate lettering of Rolls-Royce, which made no difference in Britain where a favourable 'image' was long-established, was quite unsuitable in South America and had to be replaced by a much more rugged lettering. This kind of image-building seems to be quite harmless. But if advertising can latch on to some subconscious urge and persuade families to buy useless status symbols on long hire-purchase terms, it is both misusing human knowledge and disregarding the dignity of man as a rational being. As Vance Packard puts his own attitude, he does not claim that he is never irrational, but if he is going to be irrational he wants to decide himself and not have a stranger decide for him.

The Christian is likely to be at a disadvantage where he is faced by competitors' claims which he does not think it right to match. The more such claims can be cut down to size, the more the honest trade will benefit. The only question about the various attempts to bring some standards and objective judgment into the field of consumer buying is whether they do their job effectively. There are various hall-mark and kite-mark schemes, including one for houses. There is some legislation on descriptions. There are road-tests in motoring magazines which carry advertising for the same cars, but whose warnings are perfectly clear to the practised reader. 'On the model tested the brakes did not work. We understand that this has been rectified on subsequent models.' Finally, in the last few years, have come the consumers' tests, with the forthright *Which?*, magazine of the Consumers' Association, well in the lead. This is independent of all manufacturers and advertisers, and though it touches only a tiny fraction of the buying public in its circulation, it is increasingly quoted by the popular papers. No doubt the purchase by *Which?* of the odd faulty product of a small manufacturer, or a biased report, could spell catastrophe. The more power such a magazine has, the more its integrity must be guarded and guaranteed. But it certainly seems to be a useful step in the direction of a more informed and sophisticated buying public, which is the ultimate safeguard against abuses in advertising and promotion.

The market-place is a hard school, not least for the Christian. But it is wrong to lift up our skirts and withdraw to the cloister. In other generations, Christians have engaged in trade and have, by refusing the prevailing customs and setting their own instead, produced a level of trust between men in their commercial dealings which was not there before. It is in the creation of a positive trust between men that the Christian has made his greatest contribution. The destruction of trust is the real loss caused by bribery and unfair and harsh trading. It is only if enough men are honest and fair that trade can grow, and prosperity with it. This should be a proper object for Christians of our own generation.

CHAPTER NINE

MAKING MONEY ON THE STOCK EXCHANGE

ASK the average man whether there is a difference between a flutter on the Stock Exchange and a flutter on the dogs and he will probably say that there is not. Ask the average stockbroker whether the Stock Exchange performs a useful social function and he will almost certainly say that it does. Which is right, one, both or neither?

Most Christians will agree that institutions, financial or otherwise, should have a useful social function. Most Christians would probably also agree that a useful social function should not be carried out in a way which had anti-social consequences, direct or indirect.

There can be little doubt that, in a market economy, the Stock Exchange fulfils a necessary function. The underlying purpose of all financial institutions is to put savings to the most productive use. Cash in the pocket or in the stocking has an immediate claim on consumption. As soon as this cash is put into a financial institution the individual waives some part of his immediate claim on it and it becomes available in one way or another for productive investment. The terms on which it goes into the financial institution determine the extent to which it can be committed to productive investment and the extent, on the other hand, of the lender's continuing claim on it. Deposits in banks, for instance, are available on demand, so bank overdrafts are called on demand. Time deposits are callable at a week's notice, giving a little more freedom to the bank in their lending. The skilled banker makes certain that the calls made on him can be matched by the calls he is able to make, in turn, on those who borrow from him. A banker can lend to finance the borrower's liquid assets like stocks and debts, but he cannot use more than a limited amount of this to finance long-term investment in buildings and machines. If he did, he might be caught in the position where he could not raise the quick money to repay calls made on him by depositors.

For long-term investment other terms and institutions are necessary. There are, broadly, two kinds, investment in long-term loans and investment in risk-bearing stock. The first is repaid only at the end of the term and the second is normally not repayable at any time. Without the supplementary institution of the Stock Exchange, the investor would have lost all access to his capital, and there would be a severe limit to the amount of capital people would be prepared to put into long-term investment on these terms. One of the primary functions of the Stock Exchange is to combine the needs of industry for long-term investment with the desire of the investor to have ready access to his capital should he need it. This it does by providing a day-to-day market for both loans and risk-bearing stock.

The second function of the Stock Exchange is the assessment of the economic worth of one investment against another. It must assess the management, the likely demand for the product, the availability of existing supplies and any other factor which should influence the investor in putting his savings into a particular company or lending to a particular government. The professional name for those who specialize in this function is 'investment analyst' and, as industry becomes more complex and more highly capitalized, the demands on their skill are increasing.

The market in shares is determined by the interplay of these two functions. When more people want their money back than want to put it in, share prices tend to go down; and when there are more investors, prices tend to go up. But when the market is in balance, you can almost always get your money back without loss. Even if it is not quite in balance, the decline in prices tends to attract buyers just as an increase attracts sellers, and this prevents the shares from becoming too expensive for the new investor to buy.

When the investors judge that a company has good management or an exceptional demand for its products, then the market tends to mark the price up relative to its current earnings. Instead of showing a dividend yield of 6 per cent, it may show one of 3 per cent, and this will make a share which was worth £1 worth £2 in the market. But if a company is judged to have poor management or to be in an industry where there is too much capacity in relation to demand, the price will tend to go down relative to earnings.

These price movements have a usefulness to the economy in general. Where a price is marked up, it becomes more economic for a company to raise new capital, and where it is marked down, it becomes more difficult. The incoming funds are thus set off in the direction of companies with better management and with a higher demand for their products, and are discouraged from moving in the direction of companies with poor management. The market can, of course, be wrong, but it represents the cumulative judgment of thousands of different people, and judgments furthermore that they have been prepared to back with their savings.

The mechanism of the capital market is not ideal. It tends to take, perhaps, rather too short-term a view, and still tends to be taken in by the glamour of a particular industry or country at a particular time. But this only reflects the moods of human nature and the lack of information. There is little doubt that it performs a service of considerable magnitude and that it is run, by and large, by able and honourable men. Why is it then that the Stock Exchange is regarded with such suspicion and even hostility by many people?

First of all there is a sense in which the money market is amoral. Its integrity in dealing with other people's money is beyond question. But it is not set up to be a judge of the social consequences of investment. If there is a demand for cigarettes and beer, it will steer the money very efficiently in the direction of tobacco and breweries. If there is a demand for ice-cream, the market will supply the money to make it, regardless of the numbers of people in the country still living in the slums. If a take-over bidder 'offers to purchase', the market will not normally ask how he is going to look after long-service employees. Price is the deciding factor. All this can be made to look very callous and selfish.

The stockbroker would almost certainly reply that moral judgments were not his function. His clients made the moral judgments and he acted on their instructions. If he did not, they would go elsewhere. If over-riding social considerations came in, then that was up to the government. They were the judges as to what was anti-social and as to what should be made illegal. They could no more refuse to deal in a company's shares than the railways, as common carriers, could refuse to carry their merchandise. There is a good deal in this argument. The Stock Exchange is not set up to deliver moral judgments. If there appeared to be a demand for a product and the Stock Exchange became stuffy and refused to deal in the shares of the manufacturers or distributors, there would very soon be an outcry and people would ask who they thought they were to set themselves up as authorities in such matters. But this is not the whole answer.

Although the Stock Exchange as a whole probably should not refuse to deal in the shares of an industry of doubtful social value, there is nothing to compel an individual broker to deal in them. If his clients insist, he can always send them elsewhere (which the railways, as common carriers, cannot do). If a good many brokers and jobbers acted in this way, the market in the shares would become narrower, their value relative to their yield would be lower and the industry would find it marginally more expensive to raise money. The result would be a general dampening effect on the doubtful industry.

There is probably another reason for public distrust of the money market. It is essentially an impersonal mechanism which, nevertheless, affects the lives of employees in a very real way. The worker knows that behind the company director whom he can see and talk to is the money market, remote, unknowable and far more important than the individual stockbroker.

Financial journalists say that they are very conscious of the difference between the attitude of industry and the City. Both may see the economic necessity of rationalization, but the burden of the human problem weighs more heavily on one than on the other. George Cyriax, Economic Editor of *The Financial Times*, has commented on the rather narrow life of the City. Recruited from the same sort of school, coming up in the same daily train from the same sort of rural retreat and lunching in the same clubs, they very seldom have the opportunity of seeing industrial life at first hand, and their outlook on social problems tends to be a little naïve.

The Christian who works in the City will be bound to follow the same pattern of life to some extent, but no-one should be able to say of any Christian that he is ill-informed about the way of life of his fellow men or that he is careless of the consequences which his actions will have on them. He should almost certainly take some positive action to put this right. He should, perhaps, take the trouble to understand and mix with people in different types of job, to visit his clients' plants and listen to the views of those who work there. He might even answer questions from the shop stewards on what the City does for a living!

Behind the stockbroker and the issuing house is the investor, and although the former can plead that they are only part of the mechanism, the latter cannot. He is responsible for the morality as well as the mechanics of every transaction he makes. Investment is, in general, of high social value. It is by saving and investing instead of spending that we can raise living standards in our own country and elsewhere. Investment provides jobs and makes work less back-breaking. The higher the volume of investment money coming on the market, the lower the rate of interest and the greater the number of investment projects which become economically viable. But the Christian should be more concerned than most men with the social direction of investment. He should operate with clear ground rules.

The Church Commissioners are said not to invest in drink, tobacco or entertainment. Even though a Christian may drink, smoke or pay for entertainment himself, it is generally felt that it is undesirable for a Christian to make money out of products or activities which do damage to the weaker members of the community. It may be one thing to feel that there is no harm in having a glass of sherry, but another to feel that the more people drink, the richer you will be. For those who feel that social conditions require total abstention, there is, of course, no question. On the other hand, it seems legalistic to refuse to buy a share in a building company because it may put up an occasional public house, or in a chain of stores because it may make a fraction of its profit from the sale of tobacco.

There is no major activity which one could feel certain was absolutely free from the taint of evil. And if we should not buy shares of a company with a fractional activity of which we disapproved, presumably, by the same token, we should not buy its normal products either. It is hard to believe that the Christian is put upon enquiry to this extent. It is scarcely right to spend our time and energy in straining at gnats even if we do not swallow the camel. What matters is the main activity of the company, the one on which its economics really depend.

The Christian should be concerned for more than money. Directors are ultimately answerable to shareholders for all their policies, but if shareholders are interested in nothing but dividends, it requires a strong sense of duty on the part of the directors to be interested in the social effects of their policies, particularly in areas where there are not legal sanctions to compel their interest. In practice, shareholder control is no longer effective and there is a strong argument for responsible bodies, such as industry councils, to identify the social interest and agree with companies the ways in which it can be safeguarded. But even this would not relieve the shareholder of his obligations, and until there is some such body, he has the more obligation to do what he can; and there is in fact much that he can still do.

If, for instance, all shareholders showed a preference for companies whose labour and staff relations were known to be good and avoided those where they were notoriously bad, this would become a factor in the calculations of the capital market, and would make life even more difficult for those boards who were careless of industrial relations. If, too, shareholders took the trouble to turn up at annual meetings and asked questions, not only about financial policy, but also about personnel policy, this could do nothing but good. Boards are fairly sensitive to reasoned and sensible criticism at their public meetings, and those who took the trouble would have an influence out of all proportion to their number.

For all these reasons, a long-term investment in a company seems better than an 'in and out' investment policy. It enables the shareholder to know something of the company in which he has a stake and to feel and exercise a greater responsibility towards it. Perhaps today shareholders sell out a little too easily when things go wrong. Only when they find themselves unexpectedly 'locked in' to the investment do they begin to make a fuss. Stocks and shares are commodities, to be bought and sold as shrewdly as other commodities, such as sugar, coffee and tin. But they are more than that. They carry the legal control of companies employing thousands of citizens, and to that extent they must be handled more responsibly. Long-term investment is more than the stockbrokers' 'Put them away and forget about them'.

In investing church funds, a church may not wish to have its name associated with particular political views, but this should not prevent it taking a responsible view as a shareholder in matters where the shareholders can and should exercise moral judgments. Indeed not to act where it has the power to act is in itself a decision to back the policies of the directors. If their moral judgment is considered wrong, the church will not have avoided criticism by its inaction.

The Christian who takes a responsible view of shareholding will want his investment to be under his own direct control as far as practicable. For this reason he will probably prefer to hold shares in his own name. This point applies particularly to funds invested in the name of a church or Christian charity. For instance, if a church bought shares in an investment trust, this would probably have some drink, tobacco and entertainment shares in the portfolio and this would be known by anyone who cared to look at the share registers and the portfolio of the trust. The lesson of the Paddington Estates is that the church may well be blamed even if the final use of its assets is out of its control. The church had no control over the sub-letting of its property and no financial benefit, but what struck in the public mind was that it was the church's property which was being used for wrong purposes.

However, it would be a harsh rule which excluded the individual Christian from investing in unit trusts, particularly if he were the sort of small investor for whom the trusts were designed. For this kind of investor direct investment is not really practicable, nor would he exercise the same influence at company meetings as investors with a more typical size of holding. It would be hard too to condemn such trusts for the small investor without also condemning life assurance and pension schemes, and since these are the chief forms of saving, we would need to be on sure ground before doing so. If a majority of their revenue normally came from doubtful investments, this would be grounds for objection. But these investments are normally a negligible portion of any portfolio and would not normally make any difference to the investor's dividend or to the size of the pension.

Nevertheless, the individual Christian who has sufficient capital and can, with advice, make direct investments should take a positive view of the use of his money. He can not only keep off doubtful investments, but see that his money does useful work. He might, for instance, think that instead of investing in banking or hire-purchase shares at home, he should invest in a bank which helped to finance schemes for development in the newly-developing countries.

Although most Christians who want to be responsible investors will put their money in for the long term, the 'in and out' investor does have a very useful function. Without a body of investors prepared to buy on a falling market and to sell on a rising one, the market would be much more unstable and the small investor who wanted his money out in a hurry would be in a greater risk of selling at a loss. But this is a highly specialized function and not an activity for everyone. It requires ample funds, a highly specialized knowledge and a steady nerve. In London, this function is partly performed by the stock-jobbers, and in New York by the specialists, both of whom buy and sell on their own account in a fairly narrow section of the market. Their buying and selling absorbs the first shock of a general movement in their market. They are well-informed about the shares in which they specialize and sensitive to any news or mood which will affect their market. Beyond the specialists and jobbers are private investors, who may not operate on a day-to-day basis but who, nevertheless, have the resources and experience to take a short-term position in the market. Their activities should also, at least in theory, provide a steadying influence.

But it by no means follows that what is right for the specialist is right for the man in the street. Where the specialists take a carefully calculated risk, the man in the street may be doing no more than taking a flier. There is, of course, a degree of risk in every investment we make – when we buy a car or a house or educate our children. But we try in all these cases to minimize the risk. We do not run the risk for the fun of the thing, which is the essence of gambling.

There are two ways of looking at this, first in relation to the economic function and second in relation to the right use of our own money. The right price for a particular share at a particular time is a highly complex matter. To take a view that a share is under- or over-priced at a given moment, and will shortly go up or down, requires considerable skill and judgment. In so far as the judgment is right, it will avoid the share becoming too expensive or too cheap, will swing the share back in line and do the market a service. In so far as the judgment is wrong, it will swing the share price the wrong way and do the market a disservice. Too often the ignorant amateur plunges off in the wrong direction, led on by mood, hearsay and half-truth and the market goes to giddy heights or plunges to the depths. This does no good to anyone, least of all to the amateur himself, who usually has his fingers burnt. Our first question, when temped to buy with a view to a quick sale, is whether we really know what we are up to. If not, we can hardly pretend to have any useful economic function.

There is all the difference in the world between normal business risk and speculation. For instance, a property company may have a large tract of land which amounts to say 10 per cent of its assets. The land may be without services and even without planning permission. It may still have heavy development risks. It may be heavily mortgaged. In these circumstances, the property company may feel it prudent to spread the risk by selling part of the equity, making the dangers quite plain for all to see. Its own stake comes down to 5 per cent or even 2 per cent of its total investment. This may diminish its potential profits, but it is a wise spreading of the risk. Too often, however, some people take up the shares in quite a different mood. There is a fashion for property shares or a rush of popularity for the area and wild dreams of capital gains, all of which sweep aside the cautious statements of the property company. The frantic buying and selling of the shares bears no relation to the plain facts of life. A whole lot of people burn their fingers. A small number of operators skilled in this sort of situation make quite a lot of money, there is a violent reaction, that kind of share drops out of favour, funds for house development dry up and five years later a young couple pay a good deal more for accommodation than they need have done. But for the distortion of the market through greed, this need never have happened.

There are legitimate risks which bring capital gains. A man may buy a large block of shares in a company when they are at a low price, because he knows and has confidence in the management. He may, by sustaining the share price, help to keep them in the saddle over a rough patch and enable them to carry out a beneficial long-term programme. His capital gain at the end is the reward for intelligent risk and he has achieved a socially beneficial purpose.

A lot of the speculative froth would be removed if the taxation system did not give such enormous advantage to capital gains. The short-term capital gains tax is not by itself enough. It is the artificial distinction between capital and income which distorts the market by the attraction of capital gains to a whole lot of people, many of whom do not have the information or skill to provide a useful social function.

A change of this nature in taxation would also go a long way to meet the criticism that it seems possible to make a lot of money on the stock exchange by doing very little, and that this possibility is open to those who are already rich. Part of the answer to this is that it is also possible to lose a lot of money. Another part is that it is not only stock-exchange values which rise with inflation. Values of houses rise too. But if an institution does perform a useful social function, it is better to adjust personal incomes by taxation than take the considerable risks involved in altering the mechanics of the institution itself.

Even if we do have some knowledge, we need to be careful to keep our activities in proportion to our resources. It is one thing to put 10 per cent of our resources into a speculative position. It is a very different thing to plunge the lot and, even worse, to put in more than we have and borrow the margin. The worst crashes on the Stock Exchange have had, as a major contributing factor, the forced and frantic sales of those who had been operating on margin and did not have the ready cash to pay. These people were not only gambling their own and other people's money, they were gambling with the stability of the Exchange. Part of the argument for a market economy, including the capital market, is that it is a delicate self-correcting mechanism. Speculation puts a strain on this mechanism and can only do it harm. In extreme cases it provokes boom and slump, brings the market economy itself into disrepute and encourages people to turn in disillusion to more arbitrary ways of managing economic affairs. Many forces combined to bring Hitler to power in Germany in 1933, but not least were the economic disasters in the years just before.

The Stock Exchange is not for gambling, but it is possible to use it to gamble. It is there for a serious and constructive purpose, and it is possible, by misusing it, to frustrate its purpose. In practice this means that most of us, if we want to invest, should do so on a long-term basis and after taking skilled and experienced advice. Only if we have the capital, experience and skill of a specialist, and can make a positive contribution to the stability and liquidity of the market, should we go into the business of short-term buying and selling of shares. It goes without saying that the Christian should not be led astray by the sin of covetousness. He should not come to the business of investing in a greedy frame of mind, and in avoiding these temptations he will, no doubt, save himself and others a good deal of trouble. The man who is greedy will try to get out far more than he puts in. He wants more than the rate of interest and the risk premium, and in order to get it he usually has to cut a few corners. If he loses his own money that is no more than he deserves, but very often he will have involved others in his disasters.

Whatever their faults, the institutions of the City – the Stock Exchange, Lloyds, the deposit banks, the issuing houses, the discount houses, the commodity exchanges and insurance companies – are honourable institutions, each with their professional code. This code may not be sufficiently wide to take in all the broad social effects of what they do, but it is sufficient to enable their fellow men to trust them with hundreds of millions of pounds of their savings, and very rarely is there any abuse of trust. When there is, the City will, more often than not, come to the rescue to see that the ordinary man is not harmed. This degree of mutual trust and self-discipline is rare in human affairs and makes a contribution to wealth and well-being, as well as to ethical standards, which can only be measured when it is compared with those countries which do not have similar standards and institutions.

There are still fringe operators, 'the bucket shops' which push over-valued and speculative shares. But they are both governed by the law on prospectuses, which is fairly strict, and subject to the self-discipline of the City itself and its institutions. They can be subject both to prosecution for fraud and to expulsion from the market place.

The City may lack some human warmth, but its institutions are honest and honourable; they serve their own limited, but vital, social purpose and when required by the government to comply with some wider social purpose, they may grumble, but they respond. They are not institutions through which or with which we should gamble.

CHAPTER TEN

THE CHRISTIAN AS AN EMPLOYER

IN large firms the proportion of active Christians on the board will be small; and, therefore, in the strict sense a large firm will not be a Christian employer as a small family business, run and dominated by a Christian, could be said to be a Christian firm. Even though the Christian manager or director in a large business will normally be in a minority, there ought, nevertheless, to be a standard which he can set or put into practice as far as circumstances allow. The Christian recognizes that society will never be perfect, even the most Christian firm will have its faults. But that does not make the Christian despair of bringing about a *more* Christian order in society and in industry. If we can get some improvement because we have raised a Christian voice, that is far better than washing our hands of the whole thing.

There will also, of course, be a minimum standard, and if his colleagues fall below this he would feel bound to disassociate himself from them, either by registering a contrary vote or by resignation. It is difficult to generalize on cases where a Christian would feel that he could not serve on the board of a company. If he is already a member of the board, he should not normally resign simply because he finds himself overruled by a majority on a matter of technical judgment. Even on a moral matter where a board had tried to exercise responsible judgment and the decision had gone the other way, he would not automatically be right to resign. There are, however, cases where a Christian conscience will diverge from those of others. For instance, if a decision involves the personal interest of some of the board and is acknowledged to be damaging to the company's interests, but the majority, nevertheless, are not prepared to jeopardize their own individual positions by active opposition, the Christian can hardly go along with them. This sort of situation could arise when, for instance, a minority want to have friends and relatives appointed to key positions which are beyond their capabilities; or where the siting of new plants is governed by personal whims and not by the economics of labour supply or distribution; or where there is investment of the company's money in marginal projects because of pressure of outside friendship.

It might be wrong to resign for an isolated case, but right if a clear trend had developed and could not be checked.

There is no doubt that many graduates choose professions rather than business because they feel that the professions have clear-cut codes of conduct enforceable by well-designed sanction and that, for these reasons, professions have a higher standard than business. One senior director of a large and reputable company still gives his occupation as 'engineer' rather than company director because, he says, it sounds more respectable. Even where graduates do 'go into business', there is a preference for managerial positions in very large companies which have some reputation for their ethical standards, over board positions on small public or private companies. This is not, therefore, an imaginary problem.

It is not enough to say that no-one today expects a junior executive director to take his legal responsibilities to the shareholders too much to heart. This may be true, but directors cannot be satisfied with the public's attitude to companies resulting from this situation. The Institute of Directors has taken this seriously and has done some work on codes and boardroom practice, and it seems that more needs to be done. In the meantime, those who are offered board appointments ought to take a long hard look at the situation before they become involved, and should make quite certain that the standards of the board are the sort they can live with. When issues arise with which they disagree, they should put their views courteously, but they should not allow themselves to be intimidated.

While most decisions are in fact purely technical, there is probably a tendency in modern industrial society to regard *all* decisions as technical. There is a regrettable tendency to treat erratic behaviour in humans in the same way as erratic behaviour of machines, and to wish that human beings could be made to react with the same precision. This results, when it happens, in an impression of bleak, impersonal or machine-like efficiency coupled with a lack of human warmth. The Christian should be sensitive to personal and to moral issues, and should see the moral issue when there is one and when his colleagues may see only the technical.

The Christian, as well as a general desire for justice, has also the particular command of Paul, 'Masters, give unto your servants that which is just and equal'. Anyone who has ever tried to work out a 'just wage' will know how insuperable the difficulties appear, but the Christian must at least make the effort. Justice should take into account the different kind of skills, work, risk, responsibility and enjoyment in the different jobs. Absolute justice is impossible because absolute measurement of the differing degrees of these factors is not possible. However, there are certain broad standards which can be applied. In order to avoid the evils of sweated labour, there should be a minimum wage which will give a reasonable basic standard of living. The payment of the minimum should not be waived even if the employer cannot pay. No-one should be allowed to take people into his employment unless he is able to pay them. There should be differentials for greater responsibility and for jobs which require years of specialized training. Differentials are, however, a difficult problem and it is not possible to lay down exact standards for them. But it is often possible to see anomalies, and glaring anomalies should always be put right. It is hard to justify payment to the hospital porter of a larger salary than to the surgeon with the rank of Junior Registrar. The wider the field, the harder it is to regulate the differential. But in a smaller field like a particular plant or company the application of a differential is a reasonably practicable proposition.

The Bishop of Llandaff recently suggested that instead of granting rounds of wage increases, firms should apply the amount to lowering price and in this way the whole community would benefit and not only the wage earner. After a long newspaper correspondence, he pointed out that no-one had provided him with a direct answer to a simple question. The direct answer is that this would, indeed, be an ideal way of passing on improvements in national wealth. But it would hardly be possible to apply this solution in an economy where there is free bargaining for wages. But to prohibit free bargaining for wages would be to make a decisive move away from a free economy. Even with its disadvantages, free bargaining is probably as good a solution as any other for settling wage rates. But free bargaining can work fairly in settling differentials only if there is freedom of opportunity to enter into the skilled trades and professions which claim the differentials. No trade or profession should create an artificial shortage to give its members a better bargaining position. Although the law of supply and demand avoids the shortages which would be caused by a rigid wage structure, there should be some sort of relationship between the level of a man's remuneration and the value of his service to society. The older professions, which demand a high degree of minimum skill because of their importance to society, oblige their members to charge a minimum scale which is high enough to reflect their value to society. The forces of supply and demand are not allowed to affect this minimum. No architect can try to create a demand for his services by cutting his fees. This principle of a minimum differential for skill could probably be applied more widely, and would ensure that where the public required and relied on skill, that skill was forthcoming.

Although the Christian has a duty to love his neighbour, this is not irreconcilable with the duty as a manager to exercise discipline. Discipline is necessary in all human organizations, the more so in organizations where people's livelihood and, indeed, their safety depend on everyone's keeping to the rules. If one member of the group endangers the safety or livelihood of the others, then justice demands that he be subject to discipline. If this rule of law is not observed, if actions become arbitrary and irrational, the whole group is damaged. The Christian has a duty not only to love but also to be just. Love without justice is sentimentality. The Christian's duty of love is not only to the individual who requires discipline but to all employees and others who may be affected by the conduct of that individual. The more human beings have to work together the more they require to subject themselves to discipline. The less they subject themselves to discipline, the less effective their common organization will be.

Employees are dismissed as a matter of discipline when they have not done their job properly, but also, more frequently, when there ceases to be a job for them to do. There are certain industries where it is difficult to offer regular employment, and the dismissal of the labour force at the end of the job is an inherent part of the contract of engagement. But casual labour is not normally a desirable state of affairs; most men feel the need of a greater security than is given by engagement on a day-to-day basis. In industries where labour is casual, there are ways of minimizing the casual nature of the labour, or of rearranging or reorganizing the industry by agreement so that men are protected against sudden changes in fortune. Where an industry normally offers regular employment, the Christian will want to be foremost in minimizing the effect of redundancies where these are economically necessary. Christians should also support government policies which provide for local or national redundancy agreements, since these are aimed to protect the dignity of the worker and avoid treatment of him as a piece of redundant machinery.

If it is right for workers to combine to negotiate with employers, it can hardly be wrong for employers to combine in trade federations in order to conduct negotiations with employees on behalf of whole industries. The advantage is that all competitors in the same industry have to pay the same wage, and this makes the negotiations of any increases a good deal easier for the union. On the other hand, while federations have proved a convenient method of bargaining, they have, in times of full employment, been the means of passing on wage increases to the customer and, in time of unemployment, they might be the means of weighting the bargaining power unduly against the worker. If there is nothing intrinsically wrong with them, this does not mean that they are ideal or that everything they do is necessarily right.

The rules of union negotiations are not substantially different from the rules of any other negotiation. Each side should keep to high standards in their advocacy, and there is no obligation on either side to disclose its full hand. However, the more the employer is willing to trust the trust-worthy trade unionist with information, the better the relationship ought to be. Both parties would expect the other, rightly, to look after their respective interests.

There are three main claimants on the improvements in profitability made by an individual company: the customer, the employee and the shareholder. The good manager will not try to provide for one at the expense of the others. He should try to give a bit more than the average to each of them, and provide for it by a higher-than-average standard of managerial competence and hard work.

Threats have often been part of industrial bargaining, and the Christian has to decide on the extent to which they are justified. Even if he thinks they are justified, they should certainly never be empty. An empty threat is a form of deception, and the Christian cannot justify this. Even if the threat can be implemented, a coercive threat should not be made where the act of coercion itself would be wrong. On the other hand, it is not wrong to bring to the notice of the other side courses of action which are open to your own side and which are fair and in good faith. It is also quite legitimate to expose the pretensions of the other side. In dealing with the Pharisees, our Lord Himself did not hesitate to do this. When they demanded the truth on what the basis of His authority was, He demanded, in turn, the truth on the authority of John the Baptist. They were unwilling to commit themselves to an answer because any answer had awkward implications, and this made it impossible for them to insist that our Lord gave them an answer. It is quite legitimate to put the other side in a position where they must concede the same standards of truth and information which they themselves are demanding. The quality of truth in the Christian's statement should be uncompromising, and the Christian's reputation should be such that all who deal with him should know that what he says is true and fair. His yea should be yea, and his nay should be nay without the need of emphasis.

Those who are opposed to paternalism in management are bound to take the view that the management cannot be responsible for the morals of its employees outside the time and place of employment, provided their behaviour does not interfere with the job itself. The manager's position is a functional one. His only authority over people lies in his function and in their acceptance of it, and where their actions have no relation to his function as a manager his authority does not apply.

Where the employee's job requires that the holder should command respect locally, where he has to have a certain degree of authority and standing, then his behaviour outside business hours is not, however, irrelevant to his job. If his behaviour becomes so notorious as to undermine the respect necessary for his job, his employer has to take this into account. In many cases in practice where someone has made a mess of his private life, he will want to put things right and very often the employer can rescue the situation with some legal aid or with personal advice. This is a very delicate matter, and more harm than good can be done by an over-zealous manager, even if he interferes with the best possible motives. The Christian should aim to be the sort of person who inspires a high standard of behaviour, but he should combine this with a sympathetic nature so that those who get in a mess can come to him more easily. While the Christian has no right to impose his standards on the private lives of his employees, he may find ways of helping without interfering with their essential freedom.

On the job, the Christian will want to keep as high a moral standard as he can. Christian doctrine makes it perfectly clear that there are certain rules of conduct in our relations to each other which help those relations. The Christian employer, personnel officer or welfare officer will try to see, so far as possible, that within the factory gates those rules are kept and that employees while on duty are sober, moral and responsible in their behaviour to each other.

Many Christian employers with small businesses, where they know all their work people, have taken the view that they have a responsibility to present the Christian faith to those who work for them. Only those who have a firm Christian faith can realize the desperate anxiety a man can have for his fellows who are not Christians. But direct evangelization by management can lead to the most unpleasant forms of hypocrisy. Some businessmen, realizing this, try to remain behind the scenes themselves and bring in an evangelist from outside.

However anxious the Christian may be for those who work for him, the company – apart possibly from the small private family company – is not the enlargement of one man's household. This is a patriarchal concept and is normally quite inapplicable to today's relationship of shareholders, directors and employees.

It is right that people should know that we are Christians. It is also likely, since the people are associated in companies over long periods of time and since most facets of the director's character are the subject of comment, that a great many people will have the opportunity of judging the effects of the Christian faith on his behaviour. It should not be necessary to import evangelists or chaplains in order to bear a Christian witness. If directors do bring in speakers or chaplains this should be in addition to their own personal witness. It is, in any case, quite impracticable to think they can avoid responsibility or, in any way, remain behind the scenes. They would be held directly responsible for subjecting their work people to their own particular philosophy of life. If the evangelical Christian does this, he cannot object to it being done by Catholics, Moral Re-armers, atheists or Jehovah's Witnesses in the businesses where they are the employers.

The Bible makes it quite clear that the churches themselves are major instruments for the propagation of the Christian faith. If the Christian businessman wants to see that Christian teaching is available to employees, his first responsibility should be to support the local churches in which there is good Christian teaching. If there is no suitable local church, he might establish a chaplaincy, but it should not be too closely associated with the job and attendance should be voluntary in fact as well as in name.

Some Christians have written pamphlets explaining the reason for their faith and have distributed them to employees. These have done good without forcing the employee to react publicly to the message or embarrass him if he does not want to listen. It goes without saying that whatever funds are required for this should be privately subscribed. Christians must bear in mind that it imposes a most unfair strain in a mixed society if the boss is strongly identified with one particular group of his employees. Where a chaplaincy has been created, if it is to be on the premises the request for it should come from the church or the employees themselves or both. In order to avoid abuse it should be quite independent of the management and should not take advantage of a privileged position to proselytize those of other religious groups. The Christian would be unnatural if he did not want others to hear the Christian gospel, but he should have faith in the innate power of a Christian life and of the truth of the message to make their marks. There should be no need to override sound social relationships or engage in petty manœuvering in order to get a hearing for the Christian faith. Where people are reluctant to listen we should look first not at the mechanics of propaganda but at ourselves.

If some of the Christian employees want to have meetings on the premises, then the meetings should be open. If they do not want to have them openly they should have them in their homes because, while nothing in a free society should ever stop like-minded people from meeting together in private, it is most undesirable that there should be a 'secret society' in any way associated with the employing company.

The employer should not put himself in the position where the workers feel that he regards religion as something which will keep them quiet and well-behaved. There will be those who will be only too quick to see that religion is the 'opium of the people'. What matters more than anything else is that the employer shall be regarded as fair and will be seen to have the interests of his workers at heart. There are a thousand and one ways in which he can show his Christianity in action, and in which he can be known to do what he does because he is a Christian.

CHAPTER ELEVEN

THE ORGANIZATION MAN

HOWEVER important the broad general principles of Christianity in industrial affairs, the problems confronting most Christians most often are those which face them as Christians within a secular organization. These problems all vary greatly, but their one common thread is the conflict between the unyielding standards by which the Christian considers himself bound and the demands made on him by the organization in which he works and which cannot be expected, since it employs Christians and non-Christians alike, to conform to every Christian ideal.

One obvious problem arises from the nature of secular organization. If all men are equal, is it right to have a hierarchical organization at all? Is its authority legitimate? Are its trappings a farce in which the Christian should have no part?

It is likely that far more resentment is caused by visible differences between men at their place of work than by the differences in the amount of money paid to them at the end of the week or month. The Christian is bound to question whether the hierarchical structure of business which causes these differentials and this resentment is justified, but all experience of human affairs shows that it seems to be a necessary way of organizing large-scale enterprise among fallible men. All other large-scale organizations seem to require their hierarchy. It is true in national and local government. It is true of the army. It is true of the law. A judge, at the assizes, is bound to stay in his lodgings and eat with his peers. He is not allowed to accept hospitality in the neighbourhood. It is his job to sit in judgment on his fellows, and this function requires that he be a certain distance from them. This is an extreme case, but, in a lesser way and in a more limited sphere, the manager must give his judgment in matters affecting the lives of those who work under him, and his function, therefore, requires a certain degree of authority and dignity. The hierarchy of authority is a functional necessity, both for the forming of decisions and for their execution.

The Christian will, however, try to see that distinctions of rank are the absolute minimum necessary for the function. Whilst familiarity can breed contempt, the Christian will do his best to see that he is respected for his qualities and not for his trappings. Certainly the Christian employer will try to avoid building the kind of organization which appears to need ten different grades of dining-room to preserve the subtle distinction between rank and rank. If we can make top-grade dining-rooms available to anyone on payment of an extra shilling, so much the better. Where there is no question of authority the hierarchy is probably not necessary. It does not seem necessary, for instance, where a job may require a high degree of personal skill but makes no demands whatever on a man's character. It is also probably true that the more primitive the society, the greater the requirement for outward and visible trappings of authority. The more sophisticated and educated the society, the more authority will be understood and accepted without the need for visible pomp and show. In these circumstances, too much pomp and show is not only unnecessary, it can also be an insult to the intelligence.

The Christian should realize, more than the next man, that whatever ability and intelligence he has and whatever qualities of authority he may possess, they are not of his own making. They were given to him by his Creator. This should make him humble. He should also, if he obeys Paul's command to examine himself, and James' command to confess his faults, be more aware than most of his own shortcomings and this, too, ought to make him humble. This should counterbalance, in the Christian, the temptation to arrogance, and should make him a pleasanter person to live with and to work for.

Another set of problems arises if and when the few outward Christian observances conflict with the apparent necessities of the job. The Christian faith puts more emphasis on our attitude of mind and our behaviour to God and to our fellows than on outward ceremonial, but there are, nevertheless, a limited number of observances which are almost entirely confined to Christians. Perhaps the most important of these is the observance of Sunday as a holy day.

Although the Jews had, under their ceremonial law, many ceremonial observances which are not binding on the Christian, the observance of one day in seven as a holy day dedicated to God cannot be avoided on the grounds that it is simply a relic of Jewish ceremonial. It is part of the moral law and is introduced as early as the second and third chapters of Genesis. It has been enshrined in the Ten Commandments, which embody the moral law and are binding on all men. The method of observance of one day in seven may be open, but the obligation to observe it is absolute.

What our Lord makes clear in the New Testament is that the Christian's observance of one day in seven is not to be mechanical, and should certainly not cause suffering to his fellows. From this we can deduce that medical and other public services must be carried on. Once a way of life has been geared to these services they cannot be turned off twenty-four hours in each week without physical hardship.

Today it is not only public services which continue to work on Sunday. In highly capitalized industry, particularly process industry, it is necessary in greater or lesser degree to keep the plant going round the clock, seven days a week. Even if it were physically possible, as the law stands no single competing company could step out of line. The law on the one hand permits Sunday working and, on the other, enforces competition. It is quite possible, therefore, for the Christian engineer or chemist to find that Sunday work at fairly regular intervals is an inescapable part of his profession. The Christian will want to keep Sunday work to a minimum and to support legislation limiting work on Sunday. If he is in business on his own, he should certainly limit his work on Sunday even if it means making less profit. In the old days, Welsh farmers never used a sunny Sunday to bring in the harvest and many Christian farmers stick to the same rule today. But the Christian employer, who has a great number of employees to think of, will not want to risk their jobs, and if the industrial process requires seven days' working and failure to do this would as the law now stands put him out of business, then he should not put his employees' jobs at risk. If the essence of a business is week-end trade, then the Christian is better out of it. 'The sabbath was made for man, and not man for the sabbath', but the Christian will want to observe one day as God's day and will make every endeavour to do so.

A further set of problems arises when the Christian's social life with one set of standards meets the social life of the organization which may have a quite different set of standards. When he is at work the Christian has a functional occupation which he can and should do whole-heartedly. When he is at home he can set his own standards of behaviour. There is, however, a point at which he meets the people with whom he works on a social basis, and for many this takes the form of office parties. If he is an employer, this is an obligation he cannot and should not escape, but even if his job does not demand it, he will think twice before he opts out of all social activity.

It has become a custom in a great many Christian families not to drink alcohol and not to dance. Since most office parties involve both, this poses problems. There is obviously all the difference in the world between the heavily chaperoned old-fashioned dance and dancing in certain types of night club. Similarly there are company and office parties and dances which are enjoyable and valuable social functions and, in contrast, there are those which cause offence to many people and do active harm, particularly to the weaker members. It is probably true that there is little that is erotic in a dance for company managers and their wives where almost everyone is over forty. At the same time, while certain types of dances do not lead to immorality, other types most certainly do, and while certain types of office parties may be prim and staid, others are anything but this. On the basis of their duty to the weaker brother (or sister), if on no other, some Christians do not dance and do not hold dances, and no-one can say that they are wrong. In Romans 14: 21 we read 'It is good neither to eat flesh, nor to drink wine, nor any thing whereby thy brother stumbleth, or is offended, or is made weak'. The Christian has not only to ask whether an action is wrong or unsavoury; he has also to ask whether it would, by its example, do harm to others who might not have the same discernment or strength.

A Christian director may decide that, rather than have unofficial and unregulated dances, he will do his staff a better service if he institutes an official company dance. Even if he thinks it may do harm, it may be less than the harm done by the unofficial dance. The Christian, however, should not appear to be censorious or legalistic. If he has taken the line that he will not dance himself he can still turn up to the office dance and go round to talk to everyone without going on the floor.

As far as drink is concerned, it is quite clear from the teaching of the Bible that in itself it is not wrong. But the Bible is equally clear that excessive drinking *is* wrong. Until about a hundred years ago, alcoholic drink was probably a necessity of life, but the last hundred years has produced many alternatives, including pure water. In that time many Christians have felt that complete personal abstinence might well help to raise the moral standards, and there is no doubt that in that period drink has become less of a problem than it was. As with dancing, the Christian who takes this line should not appear to be censorious or legalistic. If he has decided that he, personally, should not drink he can hold firmly and unselfconsciously to his orange juice. In matters where there is no clear-cut commandment of right or wrong, the Christian must be an example and not a cause of offence. A great many people who are not Christians refuse to drink and hold on to their positions firmly and cheerfully without offence. This is not a position, therefore, which a Christian needs to find awkward or embarrassing. There are enough pressures today to social conformity in drinking to make a positive case for those who are prepared to stand out, if only to keep other and weaker non-conformists in countenance.

If Christians have a fault today, it is not that they are not entitled to their views on drinking, dancing and gambling, but that they tend to limit worldliness to these things. The scope of worldliness is much larger. A teetotaller who spends his company's money on items of pure prestige can still be guilty of worldliness. The important thing to the Christian is that he should set his standards by his faith and that he should not be put off his stride by the views of the world.

This holds good particularly in the Christian's attitude to the problems which arise from the competition for promotion which is an almost inevitable part of any large organization. There has always been and will always be competition for office. Outside business the rules are fairly well-defined, but within the new and large business organizations the proper rules of conduct are not always so clear. There is an essential difference between normal progression up a company ladder and what is colloquially known as 'the rat race'. What goes on very largely depends on the ground rules or the lack of ground rules laid down by the company. The company can, for instance, exacerbate the competition by pressing, as some do, for 100 per cent of the employee's devotion and loyalty. This breeds an introverted and unhealthy atmosphere, and promotion decisions become far more important than they should be. It should not be assumed by the company that it is desirable for everyone to have promotion within the company as the overwhelming ambition of his life. For those who cannot achieve it, this ambition is a treadmill and they should have the option to step off it without ill-feeling.

For those who do not feel that their present job allows them to give of their best, it is perfectly proper to go on until they feel they have hit their ceiling. It is, of course, hard to know when the next job is over your ceiling until you have actually tried it. The person who is prepared to take on responsibility keeps on finding himself somewhat above his theoretical ceiling. But usually, sooner or later, he gets on top of his job. The difficulty, too often, is to find people who are prepared to accept responsibility. This is true in other professions. Many school teachers, for instance, do not wish to become headmasters. They much prefer teaching and do not want to take on the administrative chores and the unpopular decisions of a head.

When we consider promotion we have to be very honest with ourselves. There is all the difference in the world between wanting 'power over' and being anxious for 'service to'. Ambition must not become our idol and we must not resort to methods or stratagems in order to achieve it. In competition for jobs it is, of course, right to present our case if we feel that we are liable to misrepresentation by others. On the other hand, we should not always be pressing ourselves forward. In the highly competitive world of advertising, it is considered right to praise your own products, but wrong to 'knock' your competitors. This is not a bad rule in competition for jobs. A good boss, of course, makes it much easier. Most managers agree that in order to diminish areas of conflict and misunderstanding, it is desirable to have a clear demarcation line between colleagues. In this case it is a culpable abdication of responsibility deliberately to blur demarcation lines in order to see 'who will swallow up who', but this kind of attitude is, unfortunately, not unknown.

Whereas a man like Lord Birkenhead appeared to want 'the glittering prizes' for their own sake, a man like Lord Attlee seems to have been content with each office as it came along. Even those who, like Churchill, are plainly ambitious, have been prepared to put ambition aside for the sake of principle and spend long years in the wilderness. Even when in May, 1940 office seemed near, Churchill defended his chief in the critical debate rather than join those who wanted to bring him down. Those of us who have minor ambitions would do well to follow his example. There is too much emphasis today on success and too little on conduct and character. Our Lord is quite clear about this. He commends the man who takes the lower place and moves higher only when others come and fetch him.

This should be our rule, even if there are problems in practice. If an activity associated with one's own responsibilities is being mishandled and no proper attention is being paid to it, there is nothing wrong in suggesting that it should be taken under one's own wing, particularly if this is necessary in order to do one's own job effectively. People do not object to overt approaches like this. What they do object to is empire accumulation where the motive is power and self-aggrandisement, carried out not overtly but by discreet manœuvring. Most people know when it is one and when it is the other.

The Christian virtues as a colleague should not only be negative ones. It would probably be agreed that the virtue or value in a colleague is, above all others, that of integrity. The main content of integrity is honesty, but there is also an element of consistency. Everyone wants the kind of man as a colleague with whom you know where you stand, who will not shift his ground under pressure, who will accept responsibility and not try to shuffle it off on to his superiors or colleagues.

The Christian's integrity is of a very practical kind. He should never 'pass the buck' when something goes wrong. His loyalty to his colleagues should prevent him telling stories about them which in any way discredit them. Even though he should be outspoken before a decision has been made, once a decision has been made he should respect it, whether he agreed with it in the first place or not. The motto on President Truman's desk, 'remember the buck stops here', is an appropriate one for the Christian. His sense of peace which his faith gives him should keep him from moods of black despair which often affect the man who has no faith. His quiet confidence should keep him from being jumpy or nervy and, assuming that this does not come from ignorance or micawberism, he should be cheerful, buoyant, and resilient in difficult situations.

Above all, the Christian should try to give practical help to others in their careers. He should never be one to hoard his expertise in order to make himself indispensable. Everyone, looking back over his own professional career, has cause to be grateful to someone who has taken time and trouble to give him, through personal instruction, the kind of things which can never be found out just through reading books. The Christian's love for others should make certain that those who work with him remember him as someone who has been generous with his own experience.

Some Christians are unsure of the extent to which they should feel free to use their place of work as an active field for evangelism. It is the most natural thing in the world for the Christian colleague, as well as the Christian boss, to want to pass on to others what he knows in his heart and experience to be the only way of life. But very often we forget that the spoken word is only one of the many forms of witness. We are in intimate contact day by day over a number of years with the same colleagues and subordinates, and over that time action speaks a good deal louder than words, and qualities of character are known as minutely as if they were charted on office walls. Our energy and single-mindedness at work, our cheerfulness under strain, our firmness in a crisis, our fairness in conduct, our helpfulness in trouble, our concern for those around us – all these are noticed and memorized; and anything we say will always be correlated with the way in which we behave.

Of course what we do is not the only effective carrier for our witness to the absolute exclusion of what we say. What we say has its place. A flaunting of our faith on every conceivable and inconceivable occasion is wrong. What we say has to be natural to us and to the occasion. But the Christian ought to be in a position to take advantage of the occasion when it arises. As the apostle Peter tells us, 'be ready always to give an answer to every man that asketh you a reason of the hope that is in you with meekness and fear'. Not, it may be noted, with 'bounce and self-confidence'. However, our statement of faith should not be indiscriminate – 'neither cast ye your pearls before swine'. While we will not want to limit our conversation to close friends, detailed declarations of faith will probably be to those who are really our friends. People should feel that our friendship was not a means to an end, even if that end was their conversion to the faith. Our friendship should be both natural and genuine and intended to last. Humanly speaking, one real friendship is more likely to lead to conversion than a score of declarations to those we scarcely know.

While every Christian will hope for occasions when he can say something of his faith, he should remember that he may achieve more in the long run by bringing his friends to church. He should also remember that a moral life is not enough. There are many philosophies of moral life. The Christian is different from the Mormon, however much their moralities might agree at particular points. The difference should be seen but it should also, in some way, be pointed out, and it is often seen more clearly in the context of a Christian church and its teaching than it can be seen just by acquaintance and conversation with individual Christians.

We are, perhaps, advocating a much higher degree of sensitivity on the part of the Christian to the man of the world than the latter is prepared to concede in return. The man of the world is not slow to justify his actions or to attack the standards of those he thinks are being too particular. But he is not illogical in expecting better standards from the Christian, and the Christian should remember that his standards are absolute and not relative. Above all, the Christian should be sensitive to others, and they should be aware of a real sympathy and understanding on his part.

Many Christians find that one of their greatest problems in relation to their work is the conflicting demands of their work and their part-time Christian activities. Some feel that the Church is now so weak that the layman has to play a much more active part. Unfortunately a minority take this so far that they are content to do an 'adequate' day's work only, to leave their real energies free for external activities, particularly Christian activities. This kind of mental working to rule may be justified in routine work, but is an attitude which is not really compatible with most responsible jobs. The Christian's witness in his work is vital. People judge our profession of faith on our behaviour on the job and particularly on our attitude when the going is tough. People at work with the Christian tend to regard his preoccupation with church activities as no more justifiable than preoccupation with a hobby. Whatever we do, we should be able to put our hearts into it, and we cannot conscientiously take on involvement in outside activity which requires that we are less involved in the job than the demands of the job require.

This problem mainly applies of course to those who could obtain promotion. There are, certainly, examples of people who have deliberately forsworn promotion to positions of responsibility and have remained in the lower regions of the civil service or banking or in routine university posts in order to fulfil a specialized calling in Christian service and, in some cases, this calling has been very worth while for the Church. In times and places where the full-time ministry of the Church is inadequate, God may call a man in this way. But to agree to these exceptions does not invalidate the principle, and damage is done if these situations are not regarded as being exceptional. At the other extreme, of course, we must not allow our jobs to run away with us. A ruthlessly single-minded pursuit of our job to the exclusion of church and family life is an equal error in the other direction.

There are some organizations which press strongly for an almost feudal loyalty from their employees. This poses problems for any intelligent and independently-minded employee, but especially for the Christian. The Christian should, as we have said in a previous chapter, have the highest standard of work and workmanship and he owes a professional loyalty to these standards. In addition he owes a loyalty to the people who employ him. It is where these two loyalties come in conflict that he is sometimes troubled.

Loyalty to an employer does not consist in being a yes-man. Those who, under pressure, say that a project can be done for half the price, even though their professional experience tells them that it cannot, are doing the greatest disservice to their firm. Loyalty consists in the duty of care which a man who is paid by a company owes to the interests of that company as against the world at large. He must take care that his own company's interests are not damaged. This duty of care is still the same even when he has decided to leave and is being interviewed for a position in another firm. In this case he must not divulge anything to his prospective employer which would not be in his firm's best interests. Indiscretions at interviews are unfortunately notorious. Even after he has left he has some loyalty to his previous employer and colleagues. Our attitude to the firm in public should be one of respect. To criticize openly is almost certain to harm the interests of the company, and it is a good general principle that it does no good to wash one's dirty linen in public.

Loyalty, however, must not be blind. The mystique of loyalty which might be appropriate to government or to family, both of which are divinely ordained institutions, or which may be thought necessary in an army where discipline is a matter of life or death, is quite inappropriate to a commercial enterprise, which is neither divinely ordained nor involved directly in matters of life and death. Relationship with an employer in a free society is contractual. Allegiance to a business should not involve the equivalent of oaths or declarations of loyalty and it is quite wrong for employers to demand them. This kind of attitude is most common in family businesses, but in very large companies where consistent success and high standards of craftsmanship or professional expertise has produced a corporate *élan*, there is a temptation to pursue the cult of the firm as an institution. This is all right up to a point, but care has to be taken to see that it does not get out of hand. Provided the corporate tradition encourages a continuance of high standards, it is useful, but it should never become an end in itself. There is a proper sense of pride in belonging to the management of a company which is in the forefront of its industry – the kind of pride associated with belonging to a crack regiment. But too often, in a swiftly-changing world, the tradition becomes more important than the reality, and at this point it can begin to do harm by blinding management to the facts of life. True loyalty will do its best for the company by trying to improve it, not by pretending not to notice its faults.

From a practical point of view the most important decision most people have to make involving principles of loyalty is when they begin to wonder whether they should change their job. The Christian will be less likely to want to leave the company if he has been careful in choosing his company in the first place. He will not want to spend his time and talent on a business which does not have some positive social usefulness. He will want to be able to be enthusiastic and not apologetic about his work. He will want to beware particularly of going into an industry or profession because it has acquired a temporary glamour or is, for the moment, considered smart. If, for instance, he goes into advertising or television he should do so because he has real talents in this direction and not because they are more acceptable socially than other activities which are less in the public eye. We should try to find out as much as we can about the company we are thinking of joining. What sort of people does it employ? Good employers usually attract good employees. Has it a reputation for fair dealing in the industry? Are its labour relations enlightened? Is it really making a contribution to the social and economic life of the country? Is there a challenge in the job? What opportunities are there for the individual to make a real contribution?

Those who are at the beginning of their business career have to be particularly careful, because it is invaluable to have high standards both of ethics and competence in one's initial training. They should not only look at the company's trading programme to make certain that it is thorough and realistic and practical, but it would also be useful to look at the position of ex-trainees in the company. In addition, the company's financial results do give a general guide to as its competence. No employer is perfect, and it would be foolish to expect to find everything so. But there is a vast difference between the standards of work and the ideals of different companies.

But, if we do finally decide to leave a company, what principles should guide us? As a general rule of thumb most people agree that no-one should leave before he puts into the firm as much as he has taken out. This applies particularly to those who change from the company in which they have been trained. The Christian may well feel justified in changing if he feels that his present company is not using his experience to the full or if, for instance, it is obvious that it cannot afford to pay salaries comparable to other firms in the industry. On the other hand, he should not try to exploit his training and experience at the expense of the firm from which he has gained it. The electronics industry in the USA has numerous cases of scientists who have walked out *en bloc* and made their fortunes by gaining contracts at the expense of their old firms who were left high and dry. The Christian should have a good reason for leaving before he has served a reasonable period in any one firm. What is reasonable should depend on the industry and the immediate situation in the firm. He owes it, too, to the company, when he does go, to leave a well-organized situation behind so that he minimizes any damage caused by his departure.

The Christian might well have it as his objective to make a contribution at the highest level of his ability in any organization which itself is making an outstanding contribution to society. If he can do this, he will probably find that he has solved not only the problem of loyalty, but a good many other problems as well.

It is right to look at these problems of the individual Christian in a secular industrial organization and to put forward some principles on which they might be solved. But it would be quite wrong to leave the impression that any one Christian would encounter all these problems or indeed that those he did encounter would arise with any frequency. Nor do these problems arise only in industrial organizations. Industrial society, at any rate in Britain and America, has the merits of being fairly open and it is easier to move around to find congenial work and company than it is in some of the narrower professional hierarchies. But, more important, there are a great many individual companies with very fine standards and traditions, which the Christian can accept without hesitation and which he himself can help to support and strengthen. There may be much that is wrong in industrial life, but there is much good too and it is on this that we in our own generation must build.

CONCLUSION

IN this book an attempt has been made to draw on the experience of Christians working in industry and commerce and to set down the outcome of a number of discussions on problems which arise in everyday life, in the hope that this may be of some help to those who are setting out to earn their living in this way.

But the Christian standard is so high and the complexities of modern business so great that none of those associated with the preparation of this book would claim for a moment either that all the opinions expressed in it are in any sense infallible or that they themselves have succeeded or do always succeed in putting into effect the principles set out.

However, if the book has drawn attention to the fact that Christianity is relevant to the problems of everyday life in industry and commerce and that, however falteringly he may do so, the Christian has a part to play in it, then it will have served a useful purpose.

Ultimately we all have to decide for ourselves how we should act in any situation; and in coming to a decision a Christian should never forget that the principles of his faith are a most relevant and important factor.

APPENDIX

THE WEBER-TAWNEY THESIS

A T the beginning of this century, the German social historian, Max Weber, made a major study entitled *The Protestant Ethic and the Spirit of Capitalism*. In this country Professor Tawney wrote the introduction to the English translation of Weber's book and in the thirties published his own book *Religion and the Rise of Capitalism*. Other writers have also dealt with aspects of the subject in passing. These include F. A. Hayeck in *Capitalism and the Historians* and, more recently, Christopher Hill in *Puritanism and Revolution*, *The Century of Revolution* and *Society and Puritanism in Pre-Revolutionary England*.

Weber had noted that business leaders, higher grades of skilled labour and the higher technically and commercially trained personnel in any country of mixed religions were predominantly Protestant.[1] He concluded that the underlying attitude of mind of Protestants was different. Their ethos was more dynamic than that of any preceding trading system. When this spirit took hold of some members of a trade which had been carried on with a traditional rate of profit and a traditional rate of work, the 'leisureliness was suddenly destroyed . . . the idyllic state collapsed' and 'gave way to a hard frugality in which some came to the top because they did not wish to consume but to earn'.[2] The men who carried through this change had 'grown up in the hard school of life, calculating and daring at the same time, above all temperate and reliable, shrewd and completely devoted to their business'.[3]

Weber looked for the background to the ideas of this new generation and found it in the Protestant conception of 'calling', a conception unknown among either Catholic peoples or in classical antiquity. 'The idea of calling is a product of the Reformation and one thing was unquestionably new. The valuation of the fulfilment of duty in worldly affairs as the highest form of moral activity.'[4] To Luther 'labour in a

[1] *The Protestant Ethic and the Spirit of Capitalism*, English translation, 1930, p. 35.
[2] *Op.cit.*, pp. 67, 68.
[3] *Op.cit.*, p. 69.
[4] *Op.cit.*, p. 60.

calling appears as the outward expression of brotherly love' in contrast with monasticism's selfish renunciation of temporal obligations.[1] Weber contrasts the Protestant attitude with the 'hand-to-mouth existence of the peasant; the privileged traditionalism of the guild craftsman; adventurer's capitalism, oriented to exploitation of political opportunities and irrational speculation'.[2] He concludes that 'the restraints which were made upon the consumption of wealth' made possible the 'productive investment of capital'.[3] Going deeper into the theological basis of the 'calling', Weber says that the Protestant identifies true faith by objective results, by conduct which serves to increase the glory of God. Conviction of his own salvation cannot, 'as in Catholicism, consist in a gradual accumulation of good works to one's credit, but rather in a systematic self-control'.[4] God demanded 'not single good works but a life of good works combined into a unified system. There was no place for the very human Catholic cycle of sin, repentance, atonement and release, followed by renewed sin.'[5] Weber regarded his works as no more than a preliminary study, but unfortunately he died before completing the task he had set himself.

Professor Tawney's book was written in the 'thirties as a political challenge to *laissez-faire* economics and as an appeal for a morality in economic life to replace the morality which the Church had once tried to impose. The early Protestant church leaders had tried to maintain a moral code in business affairs, but the economic explosion, produced in some degree by their own ethic, had so enlarged and diversified economic life that the sort of control which the medieval Church had tried to exercise on the simpler business life of its day was no longer possible. Trade became increasingly secularized until finally in the nineteenth century utility was put forward as the sole guide to action. Tawney is most interesting in describing the kind of men who, in his view, created this explosive change.

The enemy of Calvinism 'is not the accumulation of riches, but their misuse for purposes of self-indulgence or ostentation'.[6] Calvinism 'is intensely practical. Good works are not a way of attaining salvation, but they are indispensable as proof that salvation has been attained.'[7] 'Compared with the quarrelsome self-indulgent nobility of most European

[1] *Op.cit.*, p. 61.
[2] *Op.cit.*, p. 76.
[3] *Op.cit.*, p. 172.
[4] *Op.cit.*, p. 115.
[5] *Op.cit.*, p. 117.
[6] *Religion and the Rise of Capitalism*, Pelican edn., 1930, p. 114.
[7] *Op.cit.*, p. 117.

I

countries . . . the middle classes, in whom Calvinism took root most deeply, were a race of iron. It was not surprising that they made several revolutions and imprinted their conceptions of political and social expediency on the public life of half a dozen different states in the Old World and in the New.'[1]

The Puritan 'has within himself a principle at once of energy and of order which makes him irresistible, both in war and in the struggles of commerce.'[2] In society 'Puritanism worked like the yeast which sets the whole mass fermenting.'[3] The conception which sprang from the very heart of Puritan theology was the 'calling'. 'The rational order of the universe is the work of God and its plan requires that the individual should labour for God's glory.'[4]

The labour of the Puritan moralist 'is not merely an economic means to be laid aside when physical needs have been satisfied. It is a spiritual end and must be continued as an ethical duty, long after it has ceased to be a material necessity.'[5] 'The idea of economic progress as an end to be consciously sought . . . had been unfamiliar to most earlier generations of Englishmen. . . . It found a new sanction in the identification of labour and enterprise with the service of God. The magnificent energy which changed in a century the face of material civilization was to draw nourishment from that temper.'[6]

Neither Weber nor Tawney are saying that the Protestant ethic advocated *laissez-faire* capitalism or can, in any way, be identified with it. The kind of utilitarian philosophy which says that 'What is good for General Motors is good for America' came two or three centuries later and was propounded by men who made no particular profession of Christianity. V. H. H. Green, Fellow of Lincoln College, Oxford, in an appendix to *Renaissance and Reformation*, published in 1952, deals with this point. He concludes that 'the Reformation did not cause, or even encourage, except incidentally, the development of capitalism; Protestant and Catholics remained very suspicious of unethical business enterprise, such as capitalism undoubtedly stimulated. Nevertheless, Protestantism (even more than Catholicism) may have done much, even in its early days, to stimulate efficiency and success in business. . . . It should be remembered that capitalism did not emerge as a dominant force until

[1] *Op.cit.*, p. 120.
[2] *Op.cit.*, p. 229.
[3] *Op.cit.*, p. 230.
[4] *Op.cit.*, p. 239.
[5] *Op.cit.*, p. 240.
[6] *Op.cit.*, p. 247.

the nineteenth century. By that time religious sanctions had so weakened that the Church's approval was remembered after its significant moral qualifications had been largely forgotten.'[1]

F. A. Hayeck in *Capitalism and the Historians*, published in 1954, was concerned with the easy acceptance by historians and economists, from Marx onwards, of the view that growth of wealth was at the expense of a hitherto happy proletariat. 'It was only when the larger gains, from the employment of machinery provided both the means and the opportunity for their investment, that what had been in the past a recurring surplus of population doomed to early death was in an increasing measure given the possibility of survival.'[2] 'The very increase of wealth and well-being which had been achieved raised standards and aspirations. What for ages had seemed a natural and inevitable situation . . . came to be regarded as incongruous. . . . Economic suffering both became more conspicuous and seemed less justified, because the general wealth was increasing faster than ever before.'[3]

The latest contributions to the subject have been by Christopher Hill, Master of Balliol College, Oxford. In *The Century of Revolution*, published in 1961, he says 'Calvinism liberated those who believed themselves to be the elect from a sense of sin, of helplessness; it encouraged effort, industry, study, a sense of purpose. It prepared the way for modern science. . . . The Puritan preachers insisted that the universe was law-abiding. . . . It was man's duty to study the universe and find out its laws. . . . Bacon called men to study the world about them. . . . The end of knowledge was "the relief of man's estate", "to subdue and overcome the necessities and miseries of humanity". Acceptance of this novel doctrine constituted the greatest intellectual revolution of the century.'[4]

Christopher Hill has also contributed an essay on 'Protestantism and the Rise of Capitalism' to *Essays in the Economic and Social History of Tudor and Stuart England*. He begins by saying 'Most historians would now accept the existence of some connection between protestantism and the rise of capitalism, though Professor Trevor-Roper is a conspicuous exception.' 'The central target of the Reformers' attack was justification by works. . . . The Protestant objection was to mechanical actions in which the heart was not involved . . . a Protestant thought that what a man did was less important than the spirit in which he did it. . . . For Christians no action

---

[1] *Renaissance and Reformation*, 1952, pp. 400, 401.
[2] *Capitalism and the Historians*, 1954, Introductory Essay by F. A. Hayeck, p. 16.
[3] *Op.cit.*, p. 18.
[4] *The Century of Revolution 1603-1714*, 1961, pp. 92-94.

can be casual or perfunctory, the most trivial detail of our daily life should be performed to the glory of God; should be irradiated with a conscious co-operation with God's purposes.'[1] 'It was in fact the labour of generations of God-fearing Puritans that made England the leading industrial nation in the world.'[2]

In *The Intellectual Origins of the English Revolution*, published in 1965, Christopher Hill looks at the connection between the Puritans, the Parliamentarians and science,[3] and in his study of Francis Bacon finds all three closely interwoven. Bacon wanted the advance of science by planning and direction, not by 'blind and stupid' methods which were 'more like "a kind of hunting by scent than a science"'.[4] 'The further discovering of knowledge' was part of God's plan and 'scientific investigation not only did not conflict with divinity but was positively virtuous'.[5]

Bacon inherited from his pious parents and imbibed from the world around him Calvinist assumptions about the priority of faith over reason—as well as about the necessity for strenuous effort. 'All knowledge is to be limited by religion.' 'If any man shall think by view and enquiry into these sensible and material things, to attain to any light for the revealing of the nature or the will of God; he shall dangerously abuse himself. Approaching and intruding into God's secrets and mysteries' was the cause of the Fall . . . 'Let us never think or maintain that a man can search too far . . . in the book of God's word or in the book of God's works . . . but . . . let men beware . . . that they do not unwisely mingle or confound these learnings together.'[6]

'This subsumes a long trend in Protestant thought, from Luther onwards, which equated charity with works done with intent to benefit the commonwealth or mankind; and so Bacon's separation of science from religion, so vital for the future advance of science, was in the best Protestant tradition.' 'Bacon gave the scientists' activities a moral sanction. . . . Religion . . . instead of opposing science "should clearly protect all increase in natural knowledge".' 'This religious element . . . was genuine. . . Bacon was not separating religion and science because he was a secret atheist. . . . The separation sprang from his Protestant beliefs. . . . Calvin himself assumed

t

[1] F. J. Fisher (ed.), *Essays in the Economic and Social History of Tudor and Stuart England*, 1961, pp. 16-21.

[2] *Op.cit.*, p. 31.

[3] C. Hill, *Intellectual Origins of the English Revolution*, 1965, p. 106.

[4] *Op.cit.*, pp. 86f.

[5] *Op.cit.*, p. 87.

[6] *Op.cit.*, p. 91.

the importance of final and formal causes and gave unusual significance to material and efficient causes.'[1]

'Bacon's emphasis on secondary causes ... fortified and gave deeper significance to the Parliamentarian preference for the rule of law against arbitrariness. A similar emphasis on the law-abiding nature of the universe can be seen in the dominant school of Puritan theologians under Charles I, Preston and Ames. The new science moreover, combined respect for law with a willingness to innovate.'[2] 'If Professor Butterfield is right to regard the emergence of a new scientific civilization in the later seventeenth century as the greatest landmark since the rise of Christianity, then so far as England is concerned Bacon is clearly the decisive figure.'[3]

Professor Herbert Butterfield in *The Origins of Modern Science* takes the view that, although there was continuity from the ancients, through the Renaissance, to the moderns, 'we cannot say that essentially new ingredients were introduced into our civilization at the Renaissance'.[4] In his view the real breakthrough came in the seventeenth century which 'represents one of the great episodes in human experience which ought to be placed among the epic adventures that have helped to make the human race what it is. It represents one of those periods when new things are brought into the world and into history out of men's own creative activity.'[5]

This scientific movement 'was localized and it is connected with the humming activity which was taking place, say from 1660, not only in England, Holland and France, but actually between these countries.'[6] 'Not only did England and Holland hold a leading position, but that part of France which was most active in promoting the new order was the Huguenot section.'[7] After the revocation of the Edict of Nantes in 1685, the Huguenots in exile played a key part, and as the pattern crystallized, 'it was the northern half of the continent that came to the forefront and it was soon decided that this northern part should be British, not French, Protestant, not Roman Catholic – an ally, therefore, of the new form of civilization.'[8]

It is perhaps relevant at this point to look at the economic position today of individual Protestant countries and to compare them with those countries which have a different religion and culture. We find that there is a fairly clear pattern. Taking the income per head of population

[1] *Op.cit.*, pp. 92f.
[2] *Op.cit.*, pp. 109f.
[3] *Op.cit.*, p. 111.
[4] *The Origins of Modern Science* 1300-1800, 1957, p. 178.
[5] *Op.cit.*, p. 179.   [7] *Op.cit.*, p. 181.
[6] *Op.cit.*, p. 180.   [8] *Op.cit.*, p. 181.

(*Economist*, 1963) as the best indication of national wealth, the Protestant countries bunch decisively at the head of the list, followed by the Catholic and Greek Orthodox countries.

NATIONAL INCOME PER HEAD AND PREDOMINANT CULTURE

(£ sterling, 1963)

	Protestant		Catholic and Orthodox		Non-Christian	
1	United States	902				
2	Sweden	646				
3	Switzerland	600				
4	Canada	568				
5	New Zealand	535				
6	Australia	512				
7	Denmark	482				
8	West Germany	464				
9	United Kingdom	453				
10			France	451		
11			Belgium	424		
12	Norway	421				
13	Finland	374				
14	Netherlands	350				
15					Israel	307
16					U.S.S.R.	305
17			Austria	293		
18			Venezuela	278		
19			Italy	249		
20			Ireland	232		
21			Argentina	182		
22					Japan	181
23					S. Africa	165
24			Greece	154		
25			Spain	132		
26			Mexico	129		
27			Chile	118		
28					Yugoslavia	104
29			Portugal	102		
30					Ghana	80
31			Brazil	56		
32					Ceylon	44
33					India	26
34					Burma	22

The classification is governed by the religion predominating during the main period of economic growth of the country. In most cases this does not differ substantially from the religious affiliation given in the latest censuses. In some countries the Catholic population has grown substantially in the last twenty or thirty years. Even so, in USA there are still 3 Protestants to every 2 Catholics, in Australia 3 to 1, in Switzerland 4 to 3. In the Netherlands, the Catholics are now almost equal in numbers and in Canada the Protestants are in a bare majority. (However, excluding Quebec, which has a lower *per capita* income, the Protestants are 2 to 1.) In West Germany there are 10 Protestants to 9 Catholics, but before the division of the country the ratio was nearer 3 to 2. The distinction between Protestant and Catholic is of course much finer than that which marks them off from the non-Christian countries.

Two explanations are put forward for the exceptional prosperity of the Protestant countries. One is that it is the effect of a temperate climate. This does not really bear examination. The USA and Australia are both countries with extremes of climate and both are exceptionally prosperous. Eire and Denmark have almost identical climates, products, populations and resources, but the Danish income is twice that of Eire. The natural resources and climates of North America and South America are not so dissimilar and both were settled by Europeans, but one is prosperous and developed and the other is poor and under-developed. Within countries, the Protestants are usually more prosperous than the Catholics. This is true of Canada, Switzerland and Ireland.

The other commonly-held view is that the characteristics which lead people to work hard also lead them to adopt the Protestant faith. Although this sounds a reasonable view for those who do not accept Christian teaching, it is quite contrary to that teaching. We are told that the faith is for all and that 'there is neither Jew nor Greek, . . . bond nor free'. A sovereign God cannot be limited by such trifles as national or social characteristics. But even from the secular point of view, the argument does not hold. There is no evidence that before the Reformation the Swedes, the Scots or the Pomeranians were more hardworking and prosperous than the Italians, the Spaniards or the French. On the contrary, southern Europe was much more advanced than northern Europe. The converts of Whitefield and the Wesleys were mainly from the hitherto improvident working class. In the last hundred years the Christian faith has been accepted by members of every race in ever-increasing numbers. The facts do not support the argument that certain social or racial types respond more readily to the Christian faith.

Various other factors affect the prosperity of countries. War has a temporary effect, as does the possession of natural resources in current demand. However, it is noticeable that some of the most prosperous countries have scarcely any natural resources. This is particularly true of Switzerland and Holland; and the natural resources of others, such as New Zealand, Denmark and Norway are limited.

But whatever the differences between Protestant and Catholic, the countries with real poverty are those which until recently were right outside any Christian influence. It may be that the colonial powers did not promote the economies of their former colonies as vigorously as they might, but surely some of this poverty arises from an inherited attitude to life, though this may now have been largely repudiated by their leaders.

The large and complex industrial organization (essential to low-cost production and distribution) is common to communist, socialist and capitalist countries. But where it does not have the backing of the state it must operate without any form of compulsion or sanction in dealing with its workers, suppliers and customers and it must attract workers, customers and capital in the open market against the offers of other similar organizations. Large and independent industrial organizations of today's size and complexity have not existed before this century. The extent to which they should, or even can, be made democratically answerable is one of the major political questions of our time, but their success in raising living standards and in providing the governments with tax revenue on an unprecedented scale is not in question. The interesting point for us is that it does not seem possible for these organizations to grow on any scale in other than Protestant countries. Elsewhere, organization of this size seems to need military or feudal sanctions and docile labour; or monopoly powers and docile customers; or strong doses of expatriate capital and management; or they need the cream of a country's talent so that the country cannot sustain more than one or two such organizations. This may not always be so, if only because it is easier to copy than to initiate, but until now only the Protestants have seemed to want both freedom and economic development enough to impose on themselves the disciplines required to achieve both a free economy and the economies of scale.

The statistics tell their own tale. In the *Fortune* list for 1963, 66 of the 67 companies with annual sales in excess of $1,000m. were in Protestant countries. Of those with sales in excess of $500m., 166 were in Protestant countries and only 21 in others. Of the 21, 3 were nationalized industries. By no means all the large companies in Protestant countries were American.

Britain, the Netherlands, Germany and Switzerland between them contributed 58 of the 166.

There is evidence for the view that the strength or weakness of management too would seem to be related to whether a country is Protestant or not. Studies published in 1959 by Professor F. Harbison of Princeton and Professor C. A. Myers of Massachusetts Institute of Technology (*Management in the Industrial World*), compared the quality of industrial management in USA, UK, Sweden, Germany, France, Italy, Egypt, India, Chile and Japan. The first four all appear to have achieved a high standard of industrial management on a fairly wide scale and have, of course, a high standard of living. Standards of management among the others are reported to be much poorer and, with the exception of France, they all have a very much lower standard of living. These weaknesses in management seem to run to a pattern in all the non-Protestant countries and are traceable directly to ethical causes. Managers are gravely concerned with their authority and the preservation of their prerogatives. They prefer docile employees 'who will not talk back or raise questions' rather than employees who are ambitious or efficient.[1] Typical organizational structure is highly centralized and personal. There is little delegation and consequently much frustration and bitterness on the part of subordinate managers.[2] Key positions are occupied by family members on the basis of family ties and not on the basis of performance.[3] The family is more important than the enterprise. Maximum production and performance have little place in the family plans.[4] 'The end supreme and all pervading, is the family – its economic security, its social prestige.'[5] The object of the business is to provide a reasonable degree of wealth for the family and it is not felt that the productivity of the enterprise need be pushed beyond this point. All this contrasts sharply with management philosophy in the USA or UK, where it is generally held to be intolerable that personal interests should stand in the way of a major enterprise responsible for the employment and standard of living of thousands of workers.

Even Japan, which has been most successful in catching up with advanced industrial countries, has an income per head only one quarter of that in the UK. The authors comment, 'Unless basic, rather than technical or trivial, changes are forthcoming, Japan is destined to fall behind

[1] *Management in the Industrial World*, 1959, p. 164.
[2] *Op.cit.*, p. 143.
[3] *Op.cit.*, pp. 148, 236.
[4] *Op.cit.*, p. 171.
[5] *Op.cit.*, p. 247.

in the ranks of modern industrial nations.'[1] On France, which is exceptional in being – at any rate since 1685 – a non-Protestant country and yet having a relatively high standard of living, the authors comment, 'Compared to other European countries France, in the latter half of the Eighteenth Century was rich in the attributes required for an economy based on the exploitation of local resources. . . . One would have had every reason to expect France, in the Twentieth Century, to be a leader in the world's industrial growth and progress. . . . By the end of the Nineteenth Century France was in the grip of a slow and continuous regression in its capacity to produce.'[2] 'Other forces which would normally have exerted pressure for recrystallization of the economic institutions of France remained stubbornly inoperative in an economy of small holdings, an atmosphere of widespread absence of trust and an exalted idea of personal security.'[3]

It would be quite wrong to draw from these limited findings any conclusions of racial superiority or inferiority. The Protestant ethic is clearly a waning force in a country in which the Christian faith no longer has any influence. Humanism, the prevailing faith in many of the countries which are still nominally Protestant, may have taken over many of the ethical ideals of Christianity, but it remains to be seen whether, having taken away the theology, the 'why' of religion, the ethic, the 'what' of religion, will retain its grip. Only now are we encountering the third generation since the major decline of church-going. If the Christian faith ceased to have any influence in Northern Europe but took a firm grip in, say, Brazil, which has a growing Protestant minority, then the relative patterns of national prosperity and growth might change quite decisively over a relatively short period. It is, unfortunately, all too easy to imagine the deterioration which could set in here if management and labour increasingly took their tone from their worst elements. Nor is it so very difficult to imagine the results of a full exploitation of the considerable natural resources of Brazil.

It would also be quite naïve to use these findings as an argument for *laissez-faire* capitalism and against, for instance, state socialism. Socialism may or may not be able to produce comparable prosperity. It is too early to say. If it does succeed it will probably be for different reasons, although non-Communist socialism does appear to require an even higher ethic than capitalism for its success. But the argument between communism, socialism and capitalism and their variations should not turn, for the

[1] *Op.cit.*, p. 246.
[2] *Op.cit.*, pp. 207, 208.
[3] *Op.cit.*, p. 208.

Christian, on prosperity alone. The freedom of the individual is an even more important consideration. Capitalism may or may not be an unintended by-product of the Protestant ethic, but the ethic is much broader than capitalism or socialism and not to be confined to either.

Nor should we conclude too much from the difference between Protestants and Catholics. A Catholic, particularly one educated and living in a Protestant country, can be an example to many a Protestant in his standards of work and professional integrity. And deeply though we must disagree with our Catholic friends on the doctrines of justification and the Church, we can hardly be further from them than we are from those so-called Protestants who deny the deity of Christ and whose concept of Christian authority is absolutely minimal. And the really dramatic and unarguable difference is not between Protestant and Catholic but between these two and the non-Christian religions.

Above all it would be wrong to draw the conclusion that we should be Christians in order to be prosperous. There is no promise in the Bible that the Christian will be prosperous in this life. He may be persecuted, exiled, despoiled and oppressed for his faith. Indeed this is only too often the position of Christian minorities. It is only where there is fairly widespread acceptance of the Christian ethic combined with freedom from war and civil unrest that the Christian's way of life can begin to produce greater prosperity for himself and for those with whom he lives. Even so, individual Christians may not share in the benefits and may see the rewards of their labour go elsewhere.

What does seem fairly clear is that Protestant Christianity has provided a necessary element in what was, and as a rule still is, needed to encourage the development of science, commerce and industry. This does not imply that all those concerned were more than nominal Christians, but only that they had a certain attitude to work which derived from the Christian faith and which was not found elsewhere. It is likely, however, that in its beginnings in any community the Protestant ethic was promoted by those who were sincere and deeply committed Christians.

Professor E. G. Rupp summed up this whole question in an article in *The Times* on the anniversary of Calvin's death in 1964. 'So far from belief in predestination breeding an enervating fatalism,' he wrote, 'it rather engendered a robust taste for liberty, a race of free men, a crop of free institutions in one country after another, in Holland, Scotland, France and in the New World. That Calvin's teaching has some direct relation to the rise of Capitalism is a thesis more than a little damaged. But it is true that Calvin's doctrine of vocation is, more than Luther's, apt for a citizen in a world of trade and commerce, and if it is Bucer who is the father of the "Gospel of hard work", Calvin too insisted on the virtues of thrift and diligence, duty and responsibility. Without ever going back on the great watchword "By Faith alone", the characteristic theme for the Calvinist Christian is that he lives by faith, for the honour and service of God in a world the whole life of which must be brought from sinful chaos into the ordered liberty of the children of God.'

INDEX